WHAT'S MY CHILD THINKING?

WHAT'S MY CHILD THINKING?

PRACTICAL CHILD PSYCHOLOGY
FOR MODERN PARENTS

CONTRIBUTING EDITOR
EILEEN KENNEDY-MOORE, PhD

TANITH CAREY

DK | Penguin Random House

Concept Development and Planning	Tanith Carey and Dr. Angharad Rudkin
Author	Tanith Carey
Contributing Editor, US Edition	Dr. Eileen Kennedy-Moore
Senior Editor	Nikki Sims
US Editor	Jennette ElNaggar
Senior Art Editor	Emma Forge
Designer	Tom Forge
Editor	Alice Horne
Editorial Assistant	Megan Lea
Illustrator	Mikyung Lee
Producer, Preproduction	Heather Blagden
Senior Producer	Luca Bazzoli
Jacket Designer	Nicola Powling
Jacket Coordinator	Lucy Philpott
Creative Technical Support	Tom Morse
Managing Editor	Dawn Henderson
Managing Art Editor	Marianne Markham
Art Director	Maxine Pedliham
Publishing Director	Mary-Clare Jerram

First American Edition, 2019
Published in the United States by DK Publishing
345 Hudson Street, New York, New York 10014

A catalog record for this book is available from the Library of Congress.
ISBN 978-1-4654-7937-2

Printed and bound in China

A WORLD OF IDEAS:
SEE ALL THERE IS TO KNOW
www.dk.com

Contents

1 | WHAT DO YOU WANT FOR YOUR CHILD?

2 | HOW CHILDREN DEVELOP

3 | 2–3 YEARS OLD

4 | 4–5 YEARS OLD

5 | 6–7 YEARS OLD

Foreword

If you've ever found yourself wondering, "What in the world is my kid thinking?", you're in good company. Almost all parents have probably asked themselves that question at some point.

Children are not just short adults. They think about things in qualitatively different ways than adults do. Some of these differences are delightful. Because they haven't been around that long, children see the world as full of exciting adventures and discoveries. I remember one of my children, when she was about 4 years old, declaring with complete sincerity, "I love putting money in the parking meter!"

But sometimes differences in how children and adults think can be baffling or exasperating for parents. My son, when he was 3 years old, was deeply attached to a ratty t-shirt that said, "Greetings from Aruba!" I have no idea where we even got that shirt, because no one in our family had been to Aruba. He liked it because there was a parrot on it. He insisted on wearing this shirt as often as possible, including to his birthday party.

And who hasn't tried to get out the door in the morning and said to the kids, "Come on! Let's go. We're running late"? Although schedules and appointments are a big part of our adult lives, they are meaningless to young children, who tend to live in the present moment and have only a vague understanding of time. Urging them to hurry can raise tension and cause kids to slow down.

Here's some good news: Just by asking, "What's my child thinking?" and genuinely trying to understand your child's perspective, you're taking an important step toward being a caring and capable parent. Mountains of research studies show that children are most likely to thrive when parents offer a combination of warmth plus limits. Warmth helps our children feel secure, accepted, and loved; limits teach them to make good decisions and treat others with respect. We can't—and shouldn't—always go along with what our children want, but when we start from a place of empathy, we're better equipped to guide our children with kindness and wisdom.

As a clinical psychologist, a mom of four, and an author of many books on parenting and child development, I've spent a lot of time studying and working to understand children's thoughts and feelings. In this book, you'll find answers to what your child might be thinking in more than a hundred typical but challenging scenarios, along with common parent reactions, and practical, research-based strategies for how you can respond. Being a parent of a young child, you probably have days when you barely have time to use the bathroom, so this book is laid out in an at-a-glance format that will let you quickly home in on the information you need.

As you read through this book, please keep something in mind: You are the expert on your child and your family. The goal of this book is to give you a deeper understanding of how and why your child might struggle and to give you options for helping your child move forward. Please view these strategies as possibilities rather than prescriptions and use only those that make sense for you. Every child is unique, and nobody knows your child and your family better than you do.

Warm wishes,

Eileen Kennedy-Moore, PhD

EILEEN KENNEDY-MOORE, PhD

Introduction

What's My Child Thinking? helps you see the world from your child's point of view while also considering your perspective as a parent. It is designed to help you interpret your child's behavior quickly and accurately.

On the journey through parenting, there will always be flash points. This book is designed to compress the most relevant child psychology, neuroscience, and best practice into grab-and-go sections so you can access the information you need in the moment. But in addition to advice you can use right away, this book recognizes that some situations need ongoing solutions. So each scenario also comes with tips on what to do in the longer term.

Tuning in to developmental stages

The book covers children from ages 2 to 7—formative years when children start to explore the wider world, master language, make friends, and assert their independence.

So you can tune in to your child's innermost thoughts whatever his age, the chapters are clearly divided into three main age groups:

- **2–3 years old**
- **4–5 years old**
- **6–7 years old**

to align as closely as possible with key developmental stages. In the same way you watched as your baby learned to first sit up, then stand, and then walk, the stages of cognitive, social, and emotional development also tend to take place in the same order. That said, every child is unique, so while these developments may happen roughly consecutively, children will also go through these stages at their own pace in their own way.

Boys, girls, moms, dads, and more

We have used "he" and "she" alternately throughout the book, but the topics and strategies are relevant for children and parents of any gender. Gender roles have become more fluid, and families can take many forms. Parents might be single, married, divorced, remarried, gay, straight, trans...and they provide the care that children need in various ways. Although the book talks about moms and dads, it's designed to be useful for anyone who wants to understand children better, including grandparents, teachers, and childcare providers.

Tapping in to the psychology

The book's format of more than 100 everyday scenarios allows you to quickly discover the explanations behind what your child is saying and thinking, while also empathizing with your own possible feelings as the parent in that situation.

This book offers explanations and suggestions that will help you address common parenting challenges, such as handling whining, dealing with screens, or getting kids to listen. You'll learn

" "

EMPATHY AND UNDERSTANDING HELPS US GUIDE OUR CHILDREN. THROUGH OUR DAILY INTERACTIONS, WE TEACH THEM HOW TO COPE, COMMUNICATE, AND CONNECT.

what's going through your child's mind as well as ways to respond that will help your child learn to cope with feelings, solve problems, and build strong relationships.

The structure of the scenarios allows you to find the information you need quickly to resolve any situation you find yourself in. By applying the best solution on how to respond, your knowledge of your child and his developmental stage and how to behave in similar scenarios will expand, and with this will come a newfound confidence.

Occasionally there are subtly different forms of child behavior, such as self-protective lies versus wishful thinking lies, that need to be addressed in different ways. We've put these in flowcharts to help you spot how they differ and give ou lots of options for how to respond.

Scattered throughout the book are topics that distill the best practice on some of the most common parenting issues—such as eating out, sleep difficulties, and car journeys—into an at-a-glance practical guide, with specific advice for each age group.

Your relationship is key

Understanding what your child is thinking makes you better equipped to handle some of the more challenging moments of parenting—and helps you forge a deep sense of connection with your child, now and in the years to come.

CHAPTER 1

What do you want for **your child?**

Your own childhood experience

Based on our own experiences growing up, we each bring to the job of being a parent a unique constellation of hopes, worries, and beliefs. You may want to give your child the same positive parenting you had, or you may feel determined to do things much differently.

To help understand your parenting style, use the following questions as prompts to describe feelings about your childhood; ask any co-parent to do the same. Talk through them or write down your thoughts and then look at your answers together. Don't be surprised if this brings up strong feelings for both of you. Use what you discover to think about your strengths and struggles and figure out how best to work as a team for your child.

Q | When it came to conflict, my parents:

- argued in front of me
- never argued in front of me
- used sniping, sarcasm, or sulking when angry
- occasionally argued in front of me then made up

Q | When it came to discipline, my parents were:

- strict and disciplinarian
- relaxed and informal
- gave me a balance of love and boundaries

Q | When it came to schoolwork, my parents:

- did not get involved
- were supportive and accepted my results
- put me under pressure to achieve

Q | My bedtimes were:

- rigidly enforced
- moveable

Q | As a child, I felt:

- my parents had favorites
- my siblings and I were treated equally

Q | When it came to holidays:

- family get-togethers and traditions were fun
- time together was rare or filled with tension

Q | When it came to expressing feelings:

◉ there was a lot of screaming and meanness
◉ we communicated clearly and respectfully
◉ my parents did not listen to how I felt

Q | When it came to material possessions:

◉ I was spoiled and got anything I wanted
◉ I got what I needed and some of what I wanted
◉ I felt deprived

Q | When it came to physical affection:

◉ hugs were given freely
◉ I got hugs when I needed them
◉ my parents did not give many cuddles

A cooperative approach

If you have a co-parent—whether it's your partner, a former partner, or another family member—that person will have had different experiences and will bring another viewpoint to raising your children. You may not realize how much your approaches differ until you talk them through. No two parents will ever do things exactly alike, but you want to try to find agreement on the big issues.

Understanding each other's perspectives on parenting beliefs and expectations will not only reduce blame and misunderstanding but also help you figure out rules and routines for your child that you'll both be willing to apply consistently.

Doing it on your own

If you are raising your child alone, then you will be in a position to decide how you want to bring your child up. From time to time, though, talk to a trusted friend or family member to help you put any issues you are facing in perspective.

What are your values?

As parents, we want to raise good kids. We want to be able to convey our values to our children so they grow up to be wise and caring and know what matters most in life. Our values can also help guide how we interact with our children.

The stress and busyness of daily life, as well as unexpected challenges, can consume our attention. Stepping back sometimes to consider what really matters to us, as people and as parents, can help us stay anchored in creating lives that are meaningful and satisfying. When we are guided by our values, we can make better decisions about where we want to put our energy, when we'll insist, and when we'll let things slide. No one is perfect, so we'll often fall short of our values, but knowing what they are can help us do things and make choices that reflect them.

Focus on strengths

Values are the things you stand for, the characteristics you want to be remembered for. Crystallizing these values in your mind—and reminding yourself of them—will help you keep being the sort of parent you want to be. Think of them as a job description or mission statement of who you are as a parent.

One way to think about values is to focus on the personal qualities or character strengths that embody them. Researchers at the VIA Institute have identified 24 such strengths that are cherished across diverse cultures. All these strengths are desirable, but you'll want to think about which are most important to you.

WHAT MATTERS MOST TO YOU?

The 24 strengths are featured on the opposite page. Use these, or add your own, if the listed ones don't capture what you want, to answer the questions below. If you have a co-parent, see how your answers compare. Because all of these strengths are positive, differences aren't necessarily a problem, as long as you handle them with respect for each other.

 For each question below, pick out the three strengths that seem most relevant:

- Which strengths do you currently bring to being a parent?
- Which strengths are least true of you now?
- Which ones would you like to cultivate more in yourself?
- Which strengths do you see in your child?
- Which would you like to help your child develop?
- What do you do as an individual or as a family that expresses your most-valued strengths?

social intelligence
forgiveness
zest
love of learning
perspective
teamwork
humor
bravery
gratitude
curiosity
leadership

PARENTING VALUES

modesty
open-mindedness
love
appreciation of beauty
hope
persistence
kindness
spirituality
prudence
authenticity
creativity
fairness
self-regulation

Be your child's emotion coach

When young children are upset, they're likely to "act out" their emotions by crying, yelling, or even behaving aggressively. It takes lots of practice for them to learn to express their feelings in words. Your understanding, guidance, and modeling can help.

Children are small people with big feelings. They tend to experience life more intensely than adults. Small events, such as getting a balloon, can fill your child with delight. On the flip side, children's negative emotions can also loom large. You may have seen your child get furious when a sibling touched her toy or despondent when you sliced her banana the wrong way. She isn't trying to be difficult with these extreme reactions. She's trying to cope with the situation in the best way she knows how.

Researchers have identified three main styles of how parents respond to their children's emotions:

● **Emotion-dismissing parents** ignore their children's negative emotions or try to get rid of them quickly by distracting children or telling them they shouldn't feel that way.

● **Permissive parents** are very accepting of their children's feelings but tend not to set limits or guide coping efforts. This can cause problems when other people are less tolerant of a child's outbursts.

● **Emotion-coaching parents** believe that the times when their children become emotional are opportunities for closeness and teaching. They acknowledge their children's feelings but also help them learn how to manage them. When parents do more emotion coaching, children become better at self-soothing, get along better with peers, do better academically, and even have better physical health.

How emotion coaching works

Emotion coaching helps children understand what they're feeling, why, and what to do. It puts parents and children on the same side, working together to figure out how to deal with difficult situations instead of the adult just trying to control the child. However, emotion coaching is not about "giving in" or letting kids get away with bad behavior. For example, if your child is angry, it's important to accept and acknowledge her feelings, but she can't be allowed to hurt anyone or break anything.

A parenting cheat sheet

A few basic guidelines can help you be your child's emotion coach:

● **Be a good role model.** Children learn most of all by closely watching and imitating their parents. It's probably the single biggest influence on the people they will become. Behave in a way that you would be happy for your child to copy.

" "

WE CAN NEVER GO WRONG BY REACHING FIRST FOR EMPATHY. TRYING TO SEE THE WORLD THROUGH OUR KIDS' EYES HELPS US GUIDE THEM WITH KINDNESS.

● **Help your child calm down.** When young children are frightened, frustrated, or angry, it triggers the primal part of their brain—the amygdala, which is wired to respond to threat. This, in turn, leads your child's body and brain to be flooded with stress hormones. At times like this, she won't hear what you have to say. Your gentle words or touch can help her to calm her stress response and reengage the thinking and planning part of her brain. If you're too upset to help her calm down, tell her you need to step away for a moment to regain control.

● **Acknowledge your child's negative as well as positive emotions.** When you describe your child's feelings, you show you understand. You also give her the words she needs to talk about her inner experiences and understand other people's feelings.

● **Problem solve together.** For example, if your child is angry, after you've talked about what she's feeling and why, you can explain that it's never okay to hurt anyone. If she is very young, you can give two choices of what she can do instead. Starting around age 4, you can ask her for ideas of what she can do to make the injured person feel better or to prevent hurting next time.

A "good enough" parent

Your child isn't perfect. Neither are you. And that's okay.
Your child loves and needs you—not some imaginary ideal parent.
Our unavoidable "imperfect" moments as parents can actually help
our children learn coping skills and inspire us to keep learning, too.

What's your idea of a "perfect" parent? Someone who always shows saintly patience, intuitively knows how to respond to every parenting dilemma, and even looks good doing it? That person doesn't exist.

If you could trade your child in for a more perfect child—maybe one who's neater, quieter, smarter, and more cooperative—would you? Of course not. Your imperfect kid is the one you love, and he feels the same way about you.

Social media and the sheer amount of parenting advice available can make parents feel like they're falling short of the ideal. If you know someone who seems to be a flawless parent, if you've been the target of criticism from relatives or others, or if your child is going through a difficult stage, you may worry that you're not up to the job of being a parent. But you are the right parent for your child.

What is a "good enough" parent?

The term "good enough" parent was first used in the 1950s by English pediatrician and psychoanalyst Donald Winnicott. It refers to a parent who meets a child's emotional and physical needs but also (intentionally or unintentionally) allows the child to experience tolerable doses of frustration. Good enough parents are not barely adequate, C-minus parents; they're parents who have faith that their children are strong enough to get through occasional difficulties. According to Winnicott, good enough parents are better for kids than perfect parents, because they give children room to learn to cope with challenges, manage distress, become more capable, and form their own identities.

Be kind to yourself

We each bring a unique constellation of strengths and struggles to the job of being a parent. Share your strengths and either accept, adjust for, or address your struggles. When—not if—you handle a situation with your child in a less-than-ideal way, don't beat yourself up. That's not helpful or kind. Apologize if necessary, forgive yourself, make a plan

◆ SEE RELATED TOPICS ◆
What are your values?: pp.16–17
Be your child's emotion coach: pp.18–19

" "

<u>THERE'S NO SUCH THING AS A PERFECT PARENT, BUT YOU ARE THE RIGHT PARENT FOR YOUR CHILD.</u>

for next time—maybe with the help of this book—and show your child that love means trying again.

Embrace your "good enough" kid

Accepting the idea of being good enough rather than perfect can also help us be more compassionate toward our children. It's easy to get tangled up if we compare our kids to imaginary ideal children or see their less-than-perfect behavior as a sign that we've failed as parents. Instead, we want to deal with the real kids in front of us, to find that delicate balance between treasuring who they really are and helping them grow and develop in their own special way.

CHAPTER 2

How children develop

How children learn

As your child experiences, learns, and thinks, she creates connections between the neurons in her brain. These connections grow and are strengthened through trial and error, imitation, problem-solving, and repetition.

Your child's learning fuels her cognitive, social, and emotional development. It's fascinating to see the dramatic growth in her abilities.

Learning about thinking

Your child begins to learn about the world through her senses. When she first puts a wooden block in her mouth as a baby, different parts of her brain register the taste, feel, and weight of it. Later, when she builds a tower with that block, she learns about cause and effect and then gravity, when she repeatedly knocks it over. Every time she does this, neurons fire, forming synaptic connections between her brain cells and thickening her higher-thinking cerebral cortex.

At first, she doesn't know that the colored cube she likes so much has a name, because your speech is just sounds to her. But over time, she starts to recognize the syllables you say most often when you give it to her—and she works out that it's called a block. As her word bank grows, she starts to organize her thoughts and construct longer sentences—so she can ask more questions and understand your explanations of what is happening around her.

Using more complex words and sentences, she starts to tell the "stories" of her life experiences to herself—which contributes to memory formation. Her growing verbal skills help her hold on to information and build up her knowledge of the world around her.

YOUR WARM RESPONSES TO YOUR CHILD HELP SHAPE AND SUPPORT THE RAPID LEARNING AND BRAIN CHANGES IN AGES 2 TO 7.

Learning about relating

The circuits for controlling your child's emotions are laid down before birth. Even as an infant, she tries to regulate her arousal and stimulation by looking toward or away from objects or people. Over time, "serve and return" interactions, in which she does something and you react, lay the groundwork for communication and social skills: if you respond to her squeals of delight as you walk into the room with smiles and cuddles, she'll learn that this behavior causes your happy response, and she'll do it more.

By watching you closely and hearing you talk about your feelings, she gradually works out that you have emotions, too. She also discovers that other people can have different thoughts or feelings from hers, when, for example, you want her to go to bed, and she wants to stay up. This understanding, known as "theory of mind," allows her to see other people's perspectives and form her first friendships.

Learning about feeling

In infancy, your child's emotional reactions are just general sensations of pleasure or displeasure, calm or tension. She soon realizes that certain activities, such as sucking her thumb, make her feel good; the reward centers in her brain release feel-good chemicals—dopamine, oxytocin, and serotonin—and she begins to use these behaviors to self-soothe. She also learns that other experiences—linked with the stress hormones adrenaline and cortisol—make her feel anxious or uncomfortable, so she tries to avoid these.

When you describe and discuss her feelings with her and talk about your own, she learns to use words to label how she feels. Her growing verbal skills and self-awareness enable her to ask for what she wants or needs. The more you talk to her about feelings, the better she becomes at understanding and expressing them and learning strategies, such as climbing in your lap, to get comfort.

Your child's brain

To explain the development of a child's brain, many scientists have compared it to a house under construction. Follow this analogy to discover how this amazing organ—with its basic and sophisticated levels—helps mold your child.

When your baby is born, his brain already has its own basic external structure—the walls and the doors—along with all the raw materials it needs to make it spectacular—more than 200 billion brain cells. But there's a huge amount of wiring to be done to get it fully up and running.

Building a brain from the foundations up

When he was born, the foundation of your child's brain was also in place. This primitive, lower part —necessary for basic survival and life systems—is also the source of basic emotions, such as anger and fear. A set of brain structures, collectively known as the limbic system, includes the amygdala —this almond-shaped set of neurons perceives danger, triggering the fight-or-flight response, and plays a key role in emotionally powerful memories.

As your child grows, the upper floors of his brain are also under construction. This level is where he will do his more sophisticated "higher thinking"— the cerebral cortex; it's the outer layer of the brain

and the most recent part to evolve. The cortex includes structures such as the frontal lobes, which are responsible for much of our intelligence, rational thinking, decision-making, and planning.

For the first years, and particularly before the age of 7, this upper floor is a work-in-progress area. Over time, through your child's experiences and interactions, these bottom and top layers link up more effectively, almost as if a thin rope evolves to a staircase. This means that gradually your child will gain more control over raw emotions and impulses—that come up from the bottom floor— and learn how to calm them.

Why the left and right sides need to be connected

Throughout childhood, there is another major piece of construction work taking place. Like a double-fronted house, your child's higher brain has a left and a right side. These two hemispheres need to work together to handle an enormous number of functions.

AT TIMES DURING BRAIN DEVELOPMENT, 250,000 NEURONS ARE ADDED EVERY MINUTE.

" "
IN THE FIRST FEW YEARS OF LIFE, THERE ARE MORE THAN 1 MILLION NEW NEURAL CONNECTIONS FORMED EVERY SECOND— A RATE NEVER SEEN AGAIN.

For most people, the left side is where more logical thinking happens and the organization of speech and thoughts. The right side processes spatial location (visually and physically) and recognizes the emotional nuances of communication. These two halves connect via a "corridor"—the corpus callosum.

The most intensive building work on this corridor happens around the age of 2, though it will continue until your child's midteens. The wider and bigger this corridor becomes, the more your child is able to freely access both sides of his brain, so he can gradually gain control over his feelings.

Completing the "house"

It won't be until adulthood that your child's "house" is eventually finished—although, there will always be additions and renovations going on. Of course, within these floors, there are many different "rooms" with many different functions. But if you watch out for how various parts of your child's brain begin to work together, you will start to see how he begins to master his emotions and gain perspective.

Milestones: 2–3 years

This is a stage of rapid change and dramatic development. As children's language skills grow, they'll find it easier to communicate what they want, which often leads to less aggression. They have strong opinions, and their emotions tend to be intense but brief.

Thinking

They think just wanting something can make it happen.

They live in the present and have trouble understanding "tomorrow" or "later," unless you tie the event to a routine, such as "after lunch."

Skills develop with lightning speed—for example, they learn up to eight new words a day.

Imagination takes off as children start to name objects and characters in their world and remember them. There'll be lots of games of "Let's pretend…."

Fascination with cause and effect sees children curious to discover what happens if they push over their block tower or pour water from a pitcher.

Memory growth means 2-year-olds say "Go swing," for example, before you've even arrived at the playground. By 3, children get excited about seeing people they know and start anticipating Christmas and birthdays.

Improved recall enables children to look forward to seeing the pictures on the following pages of their favorite books, which they enjoy reading over and over.

Relating

At 2, their favorite words to say are "no" and "mine."

They're able to understand many more words than they can say. At age 2, kids know between 50 and 200 words. By the end of age 3, they know 1,000 to 2,000 words.

They enjoy playing near other kids but can't yet cooperate. Sharing is very difficult.

They learn by imitating parents or peers and enjoy helping with simple household tasks.

A running commentary is the result of their newfound joy in language. Children describe what they are doing as they play and practice trying out new sounds.

Pronunciation is still improving, but children may make a "t" sound instead of a "k," as in "tate" for "cake," for example. As many as half of their words may be hard to decipher.

Clearer speech and better connections exist between muscles governing speech and their brains. So by the end of age 3, even strangers can understand most of what they say.

Feeling

They may behave aggressively when frustrated or overwhelmed and need encouragement to use their words rather than their body to express feelings.

Rapid and extreme mood shifts mean they can switch between smiling and shrieking in a matter of moments.

They enjoy being independent and exercising new skills. They often insist, "Me do it!" but sometimes want to be babied and demand, "You do it!" or "Carry me!"

They're trying to figure out the world and run it. At the same time, they're also learning that not everyone does their bidding—and that's when tantrums can erupt.

Outbursts are likely to become less frequent around age 3, as their blossoming vocabulary allows them to ask for what they want or need.

Becoming aware of adult approval and disapproval helps them learn what pleases parents and teachers.

Two-year olds may comfort someone the way they like to be comforted. Three-year-olds respond in ways the other person would find helpful.

They may use a special blanket or teddy for comfort.

Fears of the dark, thunder, dogs, bugs, and so on may develop suddenly—and also pass quickly.

Doing

They may take pride in being able to dress themselves, perhaps with some assistance. However, their outfit choices are likely to be "unique."

Better coordination results from children's fast-developing nervous systems. And as baby fat turns to muscle, 2-year-olds become much stronger.

Smooth walking and running are now apparent instead of tottering from side to side with legs apart.

Freedom of movement gives children great pleasure; they love spontaneous physical play, such as running down slopes or stopping and starting.

Balance improves, as the right and left sides of the brain better connect, allowing children to skip, hop, and walk along a straight line.

Mastering stairs comes now as children will go from using the same foot each time to using alternate feet.

Refining smaller motions, such as using cutlery to feed themselves, results from developments in fine motor skills; they can already control larger muscle groups.

Drawing skills are starting to emerge. At 2, a child can make lines and rough circles with a crayon grasped in a fist. By 3, many children can grip a pencil between thumb and forefinger using a pincer grip.

" "

YOUR CHILD'S EXPANDING LANGUAGE AND MOTOR SKILLS HELP HER DISCOVER AND EXPLORE THE WORLD.

Milestones: 4–5 years

At this stage, children are likely to be lively and social. They love to chat and are full of "why" questions and imagination. They're interested in friends but sometimes act in less-than-friendly ways, bragging, arguing, or bossing peers. They can be caring, when they're not upset.

Thinking

Attention span, planning, and long-term memory are improving as they gain better connections in their prefrontal cortex. This means children this age can concentrate and play with toys for longer.

Short-term memory gets better, so they can recall people and events from the recent past. They may not yet have a clear understanding of what tomorrow and next week mean. With practice, children can also remember their phone numbers and addresses.

Comparison skills emerge. At this stage, children can sort people and objects in their minds and figure out how they are different from other people—and use comparison to talk about those differences.

Categorization of objects, such as fruit, by both color and size is now possible. Children will take great pride in all their emerging skills.

They can identify all their major body parts. By 5, they may be able to count 10 objects.

They understand and use more complex sentences. They can also follow two- and three-step instructions, such as "Clean up your toys and put on your pj's."

Relating

Logic skills begin. Children can now engage in discussions about how to solve problems—and feel proud if they come up with a solution.

Their ability to tell stories about recent experiences helps you know what happened when you weren't with them. They also remember stories they've heard.

In two-way conversations, children ask questions to find out more about the world. They can also confidently answer questions about themselves from adults.

Humor blooms at this age. Kids think it's funny when rules get broken or things don't go as planned. Slapstick, silliness, word play, and jokes make them laugh a lot.

Friendships are increasingly important to children, although they still do a lot of parallel play. They have favorite peers they like to play with.

They may invent an imaginary friend for company or comfort—or to blame for their misbehavior.

Feeling

They have two contradictory feelings at the same time, about the same event—for example, feeling both happy and sad about the arrival of a new sibling.

Children now have a "theory of mind," which means they understand that other people can have different feelings and thoughts than they do. Realizing you don't always know what they know makes it possible for them to tell their first lies.

They respond well to rules, hate making mistakes, and are eager to get their parents' approval, but they may also test how strictly the rules will be enforced by seeing what they can get away with doing.

Empathy develops as children learn to understand other people's emotions. They usually feel sorry about wrong-doings and realize when their actions have upset others.

Children this age want to be "good," and they enjoy helping others. They often pretend to have grown-up jobs and like to do projects with their favorit adults.

As their imagination grows, they may develop fears of ghosts and monsters. They may also have nightmares.

Self-control improves, although they're still impulsive. Better communication skills means they are more likely to express anger verbally than physically.

Doing

Balance and coordination have improved, so children are able to perform more complex physical moves—hopping and skipping from foot to foot, pumping their legs on a swing, and walking along a narrow line.

Speed and agility are on the rise as they run faster and are quick on their feet, allowing them to start and stop quickly, and clamber up jungle gyms and trees.

They generally use the bathroom without help. Their fine motor skills are now becoming developed enough for them to dress themselves, although shoelaces and buttons are still problematic.

Holding a pencil with an adult grip is common in most children at this stage. They can copy a circle, square, and a triangle as well as print their name and most of the letters of the alphabet.

Recognizable drawings appear. They now add details, such as mouths, noses, and eyes on drawings of people. Coloring in also becomes neater and nearer the lines.

YOUR CHILD IS STARTING TO FIGURE OUT HOW TO PLAY WITH PEERS AS WELL AS HOW HIS BEHAVIOR AFFECTS OTHERS.

Milestones: 6–7 years

As children move into the school years, their feelings start to become more volatile again. They can become easily upset and even have tantrums. They may quit or cheat at games or sulk if they feel criticized. They may have a best friend, but friendships often shift.

Thinking

At this age, children's thinking tends to be more organized and logical. Their planning and memory skills show more similarities than differences with adult thinking.

Concentration span expands so that by the end of this phase children are able to focus for 15–30 minutes on new or interesting tasks.

They still need a lot of adult direction, and they tend to ask a lot of questions to make sure they are doing things the right way.

A love of reading starts in earnest now that children can decode words for themselves. They are likely to start enjoying reading books with more complex story lines—and may be happy to read on their own.

Writing gives them an exciting new way to express themselves. They may enjoy writing stories or writing notes for friends or family members.

A good grasp of numbers means most 6-year-olds can count up to 200 and backward from 20. Most 7-year-olds will be able to perform simple calculations in their heads. Plus, they can learn to read time from a clock.

Relating

They care deeply about having friends and enjoy sharing treats or toys with them. They can imagine another person's point of view, so they're learning to be tactful, but conflict with peers is still frequent.

They may try to bargain, saying, "I'll be your best friend if…" or "I won't be your friend if…" It's common for 7-year olds to say, "Nobody likes me."

They're aware of unwritten social rules, such as what counts as "babyish," "boyish," or "girlish."

Children know right from wrong, and they try to follow the rules. They're very concerned about fairness.

Their elaborate role-play games involve scenarios such as getting married or being zookeepers.

Competitive play begins. Children may enjoy games with more rules and care about who wins and loses. They tend to be poor sports about losing and often cheat.

Puns and word play delight children now that they are more able to understand the double meanings of words; jokes and word games are popular.

Feeling

Self-conscious and very sensitive to criticism, they may give up easily if they feel overwhelmed by expectations of behavior from parents or teachers.

Privacy concerns may appear as children begin to want to keep some of their thoughts "secret" or confide only in a close friend (who is likely to blab). They may also start to want privacy for their body, preferring to undress on their own or lock the door in the bathroom.

They can be moody, easily upset, and tend to complain. Aches and pains are common and may be a sign of stress or tension. They're likely to respond to teasing with anger or tears. Body image issues may start.

Worries focus mostly on tests and friendship issues. However, they may experience fears about "bad people" or getting hurt in a car accident. Seven-year olds may talk about death or spooky stories—or feel frightened when their peers do.

Their first self-critical thoughts may occur if they believe they aren't measuring up to expectations—their own, peers', or adults'.

Structure and routine give them a sense of familiarity and security that can help them manage feelings, but they're also excited about treats and surprises.

Doing

With their core fine and gross motor skills in place, kids are drawn to activities they think they're good at and that their friends do, too. They may also enjoy showing off their growing skills.

Children's strength and stamina mean that they start to excel at whole-body activities—for example, gymnastics, dance, swimming, skateboarding, or soccer—but some skills, such as throwing, catching, and kicking, are still emerging.

They may be interested in music, learning the words and melodies of songs, or even beginning to study an instrument. Arts and crafts can also become a passion.

At this age, kids often have their hands in their mouths, wiggling loose teeth. Losing baby teeth can be uncomfortable, exciting, or scary.

" "
YOUR CHILD IS SENSITIVE TO CRITICISM BUT ALSO EAGER TO LEARN AND USE NEW SKILLS.

CHAPTER 3

2—3
YEARS OLD

"That's mine!"

By the age of 2, "mine" is likely to be one of your child's favorite words. However, that doesn't mean that he won't ever be good at sharing. At this early stage, he is just focused on his own wants, and he needs adults to teach him this skill.

SCENARIO | Your child is refusing to share his favorite dinosaur toy with your friend's son at a playdate.

HE SAYS

"That's mine!"

YOU MIGHT THINK

"My friend will think my child is mean and doesn't play nicely."

In his home environment, your child will be particularly territorial; he wants control of his things and his space. Children this age are also impulsive. So he won't be thinking about what will happen when he grabs his dinosaur back. If your child is told he has to hand over his toy to another child, he may believe he will never get it back.

It's embarrassing to see your child roughly grab his toy when a visitor wants to hold it. But the fact that he wants to keep it to himself does not reflect badly on your parenting. It may make you wince, but all the to-ing and fro-ing over a toy is necessary to help him learn how to share.

SHARING IS THE PRECURSOR FOR CONVERSATION SKILLS, PLAYING GAMES, COMPROMISE, RESOLVING CONFLICTS, AND UNDERSTANDING HOW OTHERS FEEL.

HOW TO RESPOND

In the moment...

Don't insist. Sharing can't be forced. Studies show that children this age are less likely to learn to share if given no choice. If you remove his toy as a punishment, it will increase his worry that others can take away his things and make him even more possessive.

②

Tell him how others feel. Your child will learn how to share better if you talk him through how his visitor might feel. Say: "Joe is happy when you let him play with Mr. Rex" or "He's sad when you grab Mr. Rex away."

Praise him for sharing. When he shares anything with you, make a point of telling him how well he has done—he's more likely to do the same next time.

In the long term...

Be a good sharer yourself. One of the most important ways to teach sharing is to be a good role model. When your child's watching, ask to borrow something from your partner for a few minutes and then demonstrate how you say thank you afterward for letting you have a turn. Make the most of opportunities as they arise, such as sharing a piece of cake or taking turns in a game.

Protect his special things. If another child is coming to play, suggest that your child puts his favorite toys away and puts out only those that he doesn't mind others playing with.

WHAT HE'S THINKING

"This is where I live. Everything here belongs to me."

At this egocentric stage, your child is learning the concept of ownership. So it's too early to expect him to share what he's just discovered belongs to him. Although it's good to start helping him learn this skill, it will be another year or two before he'll be happy sharing with others.

SEE RELATED TOPICS
No! No! No!: pp.40–41
One for you, one for me: pp.82–83

"I do it!"

Your toddler is transitioning from a baby who had everything done for her to a young child who wants to do everything for herself. This move to being more independent is healthy, but it sometimes results in extra mess or delays.

SCENARIO | Your child insists on pouring her own juice, resulting in several messy spills.

SHE SAYS

"I do it!"

YOU MIGHT THINK

"This would go faster if she'd just let me help."

When your child was a baby, she was completely dependent on you. Now she can do more things, and she's eager to take charge of her world. She'll need lots of practice and gentle guidance to support her growing competence.

It's hard, sometimes, to let your child clumsily try to do something that you know you could do better and faster. But standing back and encouraging her efforts to do things on her own allows her to practice and become more confident.

ALLOWING CHILDREN TO DO THINGS FOR THEMSELVES HELPS THEM TO BUILD THE SKILLS THEY NEED TO BECOME THEIR OWN PEOPLE.

HOW TO RESPOND

In the moment...

Don't jump in too quickly. Resist the temptation to do the task yourself to save time. Intervening too much undermines your child's confidence that she can be independent.

Let her keep trying. Even if her first attempt is a disaster, allow her to try again so she learns how to problem solve.

Offer smaller steps. In their determination to go it alone, children can bite off more than they can chew. Help her build her skills in smaller steps. For example, put her juice in a child-sized pitcher that's easier to pour from or offer to help keep her cup steady as she pours.

In the long term...

Value her help. Children this age want to help. So if your child wants to put her plate in the dishwasher or asks to help carry shopping bags, give her a chance and praise her efforts.

Avoid power struggles. If she is not at risk or harming anyone, respect your child's need to be her own boss. If you allow her to assert her independence in acceptable ways, she will become more cooperative.

WHAT SHE'S THINKING

"I've seen Mommy do this, so I want to be able to do it!"

Mastering a new skill makes your child feel capable. Your patience and gentle suggestions help her persist when tasks turn out to be harder than she thought. The mess will fade in importance when you see how thrilled she is to finally get it right.

SEE RELATED TOPICS

Daddy, sit there!: pp.48–49
What does this one do?: pp.80–81

"No! No! No!"

By the age of 2, your toddler is likely to start having temper tantrums. While these outbursts can be intense and unpleasant, they are a normal part of your child's development. Your child is handling this situation the best way he knows how to, and you need to know when to step in to help.

SCENARIO | You need to go to the store, but your child refuses to go.

HE SAYS
—
"No! No! No!"

Tantrums are usually due to your child feeling overwhelmed (experiencing high levels of stress and not knowing how to cope) or frustrated (being stopped from doing or getting what he wants). Either way, his higher brain is not developed enough to deal with powerful feelings in any other way.

> ### SEE RELATED TOPICS
No broccoli!: pp.42–43
I want it now: pp.66–67

YOU MIGHT THINK

"Why is he getting so upset over such a little thing?"

WHAT HE'S THINKING

"I don't want to go! I want to stay here and play."

Your child's first tantrum may surprise and even alarm you; embarrassment may feature, too, if it happened in public. When it seems as if all your requests are met with refusal, exasperation can strike.

But these outbursts are not defiance; your child is simply not yet able to communicate in a calmer way.

Whether your child is frustrated or overwhelmed, acknowledging his big emotions by saying "You feel…" or "You want…" can help him feel understood and perhaps head off a full tantrum. With time and your help, such outbursts will pass.

HOW TO RESPOND

In the moment...

Put safety first. Make sure your child won't get hurt or hurt anyone or anything during the peak of a tantrum. You may need to clear the area or remove him from the situation.

Stay close and be calm. Remain nearby but don't try to talk to, reason with, or make eye contact with your child. If you're calm, it'll be easier for him to calm down, too.

Ease toward recovery. When the worst passes and your child starts to settle or seek your comfort, then use a soft voice and gentle touch to soothe him and encourage him to respond in a calmer way

In the long term...

Hold on to reasonable limits. Make sure that having a tantrum doesn't become an effective way for your child to get what he wants.

Create predictability and give control. Creating routines, offering two choices, and warning of transitions to new activities can avoid future tantrums.

"No broccoli!"

When you first introduced your child to solids, she probably happily gobbled up most of the foods you fed her. By 2, she's testing her newfound independence by being fussier and may be turning down some of the foods you now offer her.

SCENARIO | Your child is playing with her food instead of eating it.

SHE SAYS

"No broccoli!"

Your child is naturally suspicious of new foods, and, because her taste is acutely sensitive, some foods may not taste good. Certain vegetables have flavors that are too intense for her taste buds.

YOU MIGHT THINK

"I spent ages making this meal, and she needs to eat her vegetables to be healthy!"

Because food often represents love in our minds, it can feel like a rejection when a child refuses meals. It's frustrating, too, if you've cooked something special. Try not to get hung up on what's happened at one mealtime; she'll be getting enough nourishment throughout the day.

BY LEARNING THAT MEALTIMES ARE ALSO AN OPPORTUNITY FOR CHATTING AND TRYING NEW THINGS, CHILDREN LEARN POSITIVE ASSOCIATIONS WITH FOOD.

WHAT SHE'S THINKING

"I want to choose what I eat and how much. It's funny, too, watching the food as I drop it."

Your child is in a highly sensory phase and wants to explore new textures with her hands as well as make her own choices as she feeds herself. So she may prefer to squish the food between her fingers rather than eat it. Children play with food when they've eaten enough and are no longer hungry—and because they're little scientists. Dropping food on the floor is watching gravity in action.

HOW TO RESPOND

In the moment...

Offer less. A plate piled high can look daunting, so serve small portions and then offer more when she's finished them. Ask her to try a bit of everything while letting her respond to her feelings of fullness. Never insist on a clean plate. If your child has shifted from eating to just playing, remove the food. The next meal is never far away.

Eat with her. Even if you're eating later, sit down and eat a little of the same food. She will get more pleasure from her food if she sees you enjoying it, too.

Stay neutral. Keep your praise for eating vegetables low key. This phase will pass quicker if you don't nag her, get angry, or get upset. Research has found that children eat far more vegetables when parents don't make a fuss either way.

Avoid bribes. Resist offering sweet foods as rewards or threatening to remove treats till she's eaten the vegetables. Otherwise, you give her the idea that eating vegetables is a punishment.

In the long term...

Try, try, and try again. Research has found that toddlers have to try foods 15 times before they accept them. Keep offering the new foods, alongside foods you know she will eat.

SEE RELATED TOPICS
No! No! No!: pp.40–41
I want more: pp.58–59

Eating out

Eating out is a welcome break from the daily routine of preparing and cleaning up after meals. Restaurants and cafés offer opportunities for kids to practice social skills and understand how to behave in different situations.

Because someone else is doing the cooking, a meal out can be a great opportunity to relax and bond as a family and to chat with your child to make him feel important and included.

Being engaged

While eating out can save you time, it can also be a stressful experience if children don't want to sit still or are noisy around other diners. The reality is that it's a big leap for a young child to go from eating at home to having to be well mannered and sit still like a grown-up for longer times than he is used to. Follow the principles (opposite) to make the best and easiest transitions to relaxed dining as a family.

Be realistic about what your child is ready for and see this chore-free time as a family bonding opportunity to focus on your child, without everyday distractions.

1

Look for family-friendly places.
Start with family-style venues or cafés where there is already plenty of noise to drown out any clamor made by your own child, as well as kids' menus and more relaxed and welcoming serving staff.

4

Clear the table.
Young children are curious about new objects. Ask waiting staff to take away any sugar packets, glasses, or condiments that could be grabbed, spilled, or dropped.

6

Choose your timing.
When your child is younger, try going after nap times or during off-peak hours when there are fewer customers and the staff will have more time.

9

Select your table with care.
Ask for a quiet table in the corner—or a booth—so you won't feel conspicuous if your child is excitable.

GOOD PRACTICE

10 key principles

2

Talk about the rules.
Before you go, explain that, just like at home, he will be expected to sit on his chair, copy grown-up manners, and use his "inside," not loud "outside," voice.

3

Give attention right away.
Play games and chat to keep your child engaged and prevent problems. Don't wait for her to get bored. Games such as I Spy can help her understand what's going on around her.

5

Start with one course.
If your child is wriggly and stays in his high chair for only 20 minutes, don't expect him to sit through a full meal at a restaurant. Start by having just a main meal or just dessert.

7

Notice good behavior.
Compliment your child for what he does right—whether eating with his mouth closed or using his napkin to keep food off his clothes—so he keeps doing it.

8

Don't resort to your phone.
While it might keep your child quiet, handing over your phone teaches your child to associate eating out with screen time. Also, stay off your phone yourself so eating together is a social time.

10

Model table manners.
The best way for children to learn good table manners is to demonstrate them yourself and to eat together as often as possible. Be patient; in time, your child will learn to behave well, and eating out will become an enjoyable family time.

TAILORED ADVICE

Age by age

2–3
YEARS OLD

Let's pretend
Help children learn how restaurants work and how people are expected to behave by playing pretend at home.

Have support
Go with another adult so one of you can take your child for a walk if he gets fractious. Go back and finish the meal if you are not halfway, or call it a day if you are already close to the end.

4–5
YEARS OLD

New flavors
Stay safe in restaurants by sticking to favorite foods, but invite your child to try the new tastes on your plate and make it part of the fun.

Cutlery practice
Most children are developing the coordination to hold a knife in an adult pincer grip. Give him the chance to eat like a grown-up.

6–7
YEARS OLD

I'll have...
Children of this age are likely to have the confidence to talk to adults they don't know, so let him order his food—it's a good way to practice social skills.

Model politeness
Take the opportunity to explain how important it is to say "please" and "thank you" to the serving staff.

"Blue cup. No, yellow cup. No, blue cup."

Young children want all options at the same time, which makes choosing very difficult for them. Picking one means not having another, so they waffle back and forth. But learning to decide is an important skill your child will use throughout her life.

SCENARIO | Your child can't decide which cup to take with her on a car trip.

SHE SAYS

"Blue cup. No, yellow cup. No, blue cup."

Your child enjoys having the power to decide, but she has a hard time making up her mind which option is best. She's not trying to be difficult. She's just wavering between the joy of choosing one cup and the loss of not choosing the other.

YOU MIGHT THINK

"Why is it so hard for her to make up her mind? Maybe I should decide for her."

Decisions are hard to make even when you're a grown-up, so while your child is still getting practice, it may feel like she's taking a long time. Resist the temptation to hurry things along by deciding for her. Your patience will be rewarded as her decision-making skills improve.

SEE RELATED TOPICS

No coat!: pp. 50–51
I'm not finished: pp.68–69

WHAT SHE'S THINKING

"I can't figure out which cup will make me happier."

Offering two acceptable options can be a good way to get children to cooperate with adult goals. Allowing your child to choose "Now or then?" "Me or you?" "This or that?" gives her a healthy sense of control. But if she's stressed or tired, she may feel overwhelmed by choices.

HOW TO RESPOND

In the moment...

Give her the vocabulary. Use decision words, such as "choose," "pick," and "prefer," so she can express how it feels to make a choice.

Redirect to minimize fretting. As soon as your child chooses, move quickly to the next activity so she has less opportunity to rethink her decision. Say, "You picked the yellow cup! Hold it tightly, and let's fill it up!"

Put decisions in context. If your child is wavering, emphasize that there will be more opportunities for choices. Tell her, "Tomorrow, you can pick the blue cup."

In the long term...

Narrow the field. Too many options are overwhelming for young children. Instead of offering a wide choice, it's often best to present just two options, especially when you are in a rush.

Model decision-making. Talk out loud about the decisions you are making throughout the day, whether it's to wear a pair of jeans instead of shorts or cook a baked potato instead of pasta. Let your child hear you weigh the pros and cons.

"Daddy, sit there!"

Children live in a world where they are constantly told what to do by grown-ups. Now that your child is able to express himself more clearly, he is going through a phase of handing out some orders himself.

SCENARIO | **When you have a family meal, your child points to the seat where he wants you to sit.**

HE SAYS

"Daddy, sit there!"

YOU MIGHT THINK

"Why is he being so bossy?"

At this age, your child is simultaneously trying to figure out the world and run it. He is now able to string together sentences of three words, so he can clearly issue orders. He has ideas of how he'd like things and enjoys having you do his bidding for a change.

You might find it funny, or even cute, that your child is acting like a mini-dictator. But you may also be annoyed by his orders and worry that he'll turn into a tyrant if you give in too much. His commands are a sign of his growing confidence and speech skills. Flexibility and compromise come later.

SEE YOUR CHILD'S PERCEIVED "BOSSINESS" AS A REFLECTION OF HIS GROWING LANGUAGE SKILLS AND NEED FOR HIS WORLD TO FEEL PREDICTABLE.

WHAT HE'S THINKING

"I like things the same so I know what to expect."

Predictability and control make him feel secure, and he may particularly want the same rituals at transition times, such as meals, because switching from one activity to another is already a big effort. He wants things his way, but he's also experimenting to figure out what he can control and what he can't.

HOW TO RESPOND

In the moment...

Acknowledge his wish. While the decision is ultimately yours, pay attention to and consider his request so he knows you are listening. If you need to sit elsewhere, say, "I know you like to tell me where to sit, but I am sitting here today to help Mommy bring in the food."

Make light of it. Lighten the atmosphere by being humorous. Try rephrasing your child's command as "So you'd really like it if I sat here today?" and then sit on the floor. Even a young child will appreciate absurdity, and seeing the funny side will help him shift his focus.

In the long term...

Don't see it as a battle. This bossiness is usually just a phase. Your child's social and verbal skills are still a work in progress, so he hasn't mastered polite diplomacy. He is still learning that other people have thoughts and feelings separate from his own.

Model polite requests. Help make "please" and "thank you" part of your child's vocabulary by using it yourself with every request.

Encourage flexibility. When your child dishes out the orders but accepts it when you show him his way is not the only way, thank him for being flexible.

SEE RELATED TOPICS

No broccoli!: pp.42–43
Don't like her: pp.60–61

"No coat!"

As children learn to dress themselves, they will want to choose the clothes they wear. Their choices may reflect a wish for comfort or a favorite color, pattern, or character, but they won't consider adult concerns about weather, matching colors, or the schedule for the day.

SCENARIO | **You're off to the park and it's cold outside, but your child refuses to put on her coat.**

SHE SAYS

"No coat!"

When you're trying to get out the door, and your child digs in her heels in an unreasonable way, it can be very frustrating. Your child isn't trying to be difficult, though. She just wants to be in charge of her own body and what she wears.

YOU MIGHT THINK

"It's freezing out there! I can't let her go out without a coat!"

You may be anxious about her catching a cold or that others won't see you as a good parent if she is not dressed appropriately. But it's useful to know that children often don't feel the temperature as much as adults—they have a smaller skin surface area to keep warm, have a faster metabolism, and are more active, so don't worry too much.

" "

BUILD IN A BIT MORE TIME BEFORE YOU LEAVE THE HOUSE JUST IN CASE YOUR TODDLER WANTS TO BE IN CHARGE OF SOMETHING.

HOW TO RESPOND

In the moment...

1

Stay calm. Rather than shout, get down to her level and speak softly. If you get annoyed, it will turn into a power struggle.

2

Offer a different choice. Giving her some control can break through stubbornness. Say, "It's cold out, so you need to wear a coat." Then offer her a choice of two hats or two different but equally acceptable coats.

3

Talk about "when," not "if." Say, "Tell me when you're ready for your coat." After a few steps outside in the chilly breeze, she'll likely be more willing to wear her coat.

In the long term...

Choose comfortable clothes. If you are buying your child a new coat, let her try it on first to make sure it feels comfortable. Second-hand clothes are a good option because they have been washed a lot so are softer and not so stiff, as are looser options that she can simply pull over her head herself. Cut out any tags that could annoy her.

Remove unacceptable options. Put away clothes that are out of season, too small, or too fancy for every day so your child can choose only outfits that you don't mind her wearing.

WHAT SHE'S THINKING

"I don't like feeling bundled up. I can't move in this coat."

Just like adults, children have their favorite clothes. For children, it's often more about comfort and ease of movement. Some coats can make your child feel constricted, and certain materials can feel itchy or create unpleasant sensations when close to children's sensitive skin.

SEE RELATED TOPICS
I do it!: pp.38–39
No! No! No!: pp.40–41

"Mommy, don't go!"

Your child's basic survival instincts mean he is primed to want to stay close to you. When you have to leave him, no matter who he's with, this bond can lead to separation anxiety, which can be very upsetting for both you and your child.

SCENARIO | **Grandma has come to look after your child while you run out for an exercise class, but he clings to you as you leave.**

HE SAYS

"Mommy, don't go!"

YOU MIGHT THINK

"I hate to see him get so upset when I'll be gone only an hour."

Separation anxiety is common between 8 and 12 months and between 18 months and 2½ years. Your child protests when you leave because you are the person who makes him feel the most safe and loved, so it's hard for him to see you go away.

Seeing your child crying and clinging may trigger guilt or make you wonder if it's worth going through all of this just to go to the gym. But if you get upset, delay leaving, or keep checking on him, the message he gets is, "Mommy's worried about leaving me, too, so it must be scary!"

GIVING YOUR CHILD REGULAR PRACTICE AT BEING WITH OTHER CARERS HELPS HIM LEARN TO FEEL COMFORTABLE WHEN YOU'RE NOT THERE.

WHAT HE'S THINKING

"I love Mommy and want her with me, always."

The moment of parting is difficult, especially if your child hasn't had much practice being away from you. But if you're calm and confident, he's likely to settle quickly after you leave. Some kids find it easier to walk away from a parent than to watch a parent walk away from them. Try happily waving goodbye as he and Grandma go to the park.

SEE RELATED TOPICS

Don't like her: pp.60–61
Not Mommy. Want Daddy: pp.72–73

HOW TO RESPOND

In the moment...

Show faith in your child's carer. Your child will take his cues from you, so be confident, smile and engage him and Grandma in a conversation about what games they both like to play and what fun things they will do together. (The same approach would work in a childcare setting.)

Don't sneak out or have long farewells. You may want to sneak out to avoid a scene or stay to try to settle him before you go. Either will increase his anxiety about parting. A confident goodbye assures him that you know he'll be fine without you for a bit.

Have his carer distract him. The sadness of farewell will likely pass quickly if Grandma acts swiftly to redirect him toward a fun activity. If he won't participate at first, have her play enthusiastically. Pretty soon, he won't be able to resist joining in.

In the long term...

Practice short separations. Children this age don't have much sense of time, so it's the moment of goodbye that he needs help handling. Having many experiences of seeing you go away and then come back will help him feel more comfortable with this process and set the stage for starting school. You may want to begin with just playing hide-and-seek.

Make it predictable. Farewell and reunion rituals make goodbyes easier. Maybe give him a hug and two kisses then chant, "I'm going away, but then I'll come back." Tie your return to an event, such as after lunch. When you return, repeat the hugs and kisses then chant, "I went away, but now I've come back."

Hitting and biting

Though often alarming for parents to witness, aggression between children is a typical part of development. It's usually a phase they grow out of as they learn self-control and the verbal skills to sort conflicts without violence.

Starting around age 2, your child may bite or hit to get her way or protect her turf. She may also lash out when she's feeling overwhelmed, cornered, or even overexcited. Aggressive responses—such as hitting, biting, pinching, kicking, or throwing things—usually happen because your child hasn't yet developed good internal brakes. It's hard for her to empathize, anticipate reactions, calm herself, and think through alternatives, so she can't resist her impulse to lash out.

If your child is acting aggressively, you may feel guilty about the injuries she causes, blamed for her actions, helpless to control her behavior (especially when you're not around), and worried that she'll be seen as a handful at preschool and not welcome at playdates or parties.

It will take time and patience, but you can teach your child to cope with her intense feelings and avoid hurting anyone.

" "

AGGRESSIVE BEHAVIOR, SUCH AS BITING AND HITTING, IS A PHASE MANY YOUNG CHILDREN GO THROUGH BEFORE THEY LEARN SELF-CONTROL.

1
Put her feelings into words.
If you see her starting to get upset, wrap her feelings up in words and a gentle touch to tame her impulse to hit. Move behind her and gently stroke her chest and belly as you say, "You're mad that he grabbed your toy. Tell him, 'I was playing with that.'"

4
Do a replay.
After the incident is over, in a calm and private moment, help your child figure out what she could have done differently and then practice by acting it out. This will make it easier for her to do it right next time.

7
Look for other factors.
Your child may be hungry, tired, wired, or overwhelmed, but it's hard for her to recognize this or ask for what she needs. Consistent routine makes aggressive flare-ups less likely.

GOOD PRACTICE

8 key principles

2

Pay more attention to the victim than the hitter.
First ask the child on the receiving end if he is okay. This will send a message to your child that she will not be the one to get the attention if she bites or hits.

3

Step in right away.
Your child's fight-or-flight reflex has already kicked in by the time she has lashed out. So rather than shout and elevate her stress levels, remove her, look her in the eye, and say: "Hitting hurts. You can be angry, but you may not hit."

5

Give positive attention.
Be careful that hurting others doesn't become the best way to get your attention. It's easy to notice when kids are being bad, but we need to make a point of catching them being good. With children, we get more of the behavior we pay attention to.

6

Notice kind behavior.
Get into the habit of looking out for the times when she is being kind, sharing, and playing nicely with other children. Point out how her kindness makes others feel.

8

Create coping cards.
Put drawings or photos on index cards to show healthy ways to cope: count to 10, give yourself a hug, ask for what you want, tell a grown-up, play with someone else. Use the cards to help your child plan how to handle tough situations.

2–3
YEARS OLD

No mind reader
Young children may not realize that they have to tell other children what they do or don't like when they play. Give her words to express her wishes.

Take it outdoors
Most young kids, especially those with high energy, feel calmer if they have plenty of time to run and play outside.

4–5
YEARS OLD

Focus on prevention
Know the situations that tend to trigger your child's aggression. Stay nearby to prevent hurting and help her respond in a better way.

Practice strategies
Use role-play to help your child practice using her words or giving herself a hug instead of hitting.

6–7
YEARS OLD

Is it play-fighting?
Boys are more likely than girls to enjoy rough and tumble play. If all parties are smiling, it's just good-natured fun, so you probably don't need to intervene.

Extra help
If your child still hasn't learned to refrain from hurting classmates, consider talking to a school counselor or other mental health professional.

"Want your phone!"

Thanks to their colorful screens, phones and tablets are fascinating to children. They can quickly and easily distract an irritable or bored child. But too much time on devices can cause delays in language, cognitive, social, and emotional learning.

SCENARIO | While you're waiting for lunch at a café, your child asks if he can play on your phone.

HE SAYS

"Want your phone!"

Your child sees adults spending a lot of time on their devices, so he wants to play with them, too. In his eyes, a phone is the ultimate, high-tech toy. If he is allowed to play with it whenever he's bored or upset, he may come to depend on it for distraction and entertainment.

YOU MIGHT THINK

"My phone will keep him occupied until the food comes. If I say no, he may have a tantrum."

It's tempting to give in to your child rather than face a meltdown. However, if your child gets used to relying on a device to cope with downtime, he may become less interested in and adept at using nonscreen ways of entertaining himself. He's also likely to fuss when you tell him to put it away.

◆ SEE RELATED TOPICS ◆
I want it now!: pp.66–67
What does this one do?: pp.80–81

WHAT HE'S THINKING

"It's fun to play on Daddy's phone. I like the pictures."

The bright colors and graphics that react to the touch of a finger trigger the reward pathways in your child's brain. Electronic devices can be hypnotizing and habit-forming for children as well as for adults. They can also keep kids up at night.

YOUNG CHILDREN LEARN MOST DEEPLY FROM INTERACTING WITH PEOPLE AND THEIR PHYSICAL WORLD.

HOW TO RESPOND

In the moment...

Put your phone away. Keep texting, social media, and phone conversations to a minimum when you're with your child. Kids act up when parents are distracted by their phones. Use the time to talk, play, or draw together and model healthy restraint with your device.

Say no. Set clear boundaries about when electronics are off-limits. Avoid using them during meals, family time, playdates, short drives, most outdoor activities, or before bed. Your child may protest, but he needs your wise limits.

Think of what he'll miss. The biggest problem with electronics use with children is what it replaces: having conversations, cooperating, compromising, learning to cope with boredom or frustration, climbing, touching, building... The more your child relies on devices for entertainment, the more he'll want them and the more experiences he'll miss.

In the long term...

Don't believe electronics are necessary to make your child smarter. Starting around 30 months, kids can learn isolated concepts from tablets, just as they can from TV, but they don't need them. It's much easier for them to connect concepts to the real world when they talk with people and explore with their bodies.

Do it thoughtfully. If you decide to give your young child access to electronics, use them to explore and connect. Do it together, make it brief, and choose age-appropriate content. Try taking photos of bugs, looking up types of trucks, or video-calling Grandma.

"I want more!"

At this age, children begin to eat for reasons other than hunger—because they're bored, worried, want attention, or just like the taste of something. Avoiding pressure and excessive restrictions keeps food enjoyable and makes it easier for your child to listen to her body to recognize hunger and fullness.

SCENARIO | Your child is asking for another cupcake.

SHE SAYS

"I want more!"

Certain foods are particularly delicious and hard to resist. Eating sweet foods is a strong sensory experience for children. Their preference for sweet things is universal and hardwired from birth, probably to make sure they accept sweet-tasting foods, such as their mother's milk, and to avoid bitter foods that could be poisonous.

SEE RELATED TOPICS

Please, please, please: pp.70–71
No coloring on the wall: pp.174–175

YOU MIGHT THINK

"She's had enough treats. If she has more, I'm worried she'll feel sick or won't eat her dinner."

WHAT SHE'S THINKING

"Why is Mommy not letting me have another one?"

Allowing your child to tune in to her body's signals of when she's had enough is crucial to modeling a relaxed and stress-free attitude toward food. Severely restricting certain foods or labeling them as "bad" encourages overeating.

Your child will think there's no reason to stop eating cupcakes if they taste yummy. She may need your guidance to stop at one serving of dessert, so it doesn't interfere with meals.

HOW TO RESPOND

In the moment...

Explain why you are saying no. Stay neutral while explaining that it's important she eats a good variety of foods to help her grow healthy and strong. Tell her that while sugary foods can taste yummy, she needs room in her tummy for other foods.

Take the long view. Occasional overeating of sweets won't hurt your child, but strong restrictions can lead to sneaking or gorging followed by guilt. A matter-of-fact attitude toward sweets helps her view them as ordinary rather than emotionally loaded.

In the long term...

Don't link food with emotions. Avoid offering food, and especially sweets, as a reward for good behavior or as a comfort when she is upset. Also, don't withhold sweets as punishment, or they can seem too important.

Watch for added sugar. Many foods marketed to children are extra sweet. If your child is used to having foods and drinks with added sugar, then healthy choices, such as fruits, veggies, and water, will seem less appealing.

Build structure. To help your child experience the sensations of hunger and fullness, avoid constant grazing or absentminded eating. Instead, have regular meal- and snack times when family members eat at the table and enjoy each other's company.

"Don't like her."

At some point, you'll probably want or need your child to be watched by someone other than you. Whether it's a family member, babysitter, preschool, or day care, your child can learn that he'll be safe and even have fun with a trusted caregiver.

SCENARIO | **Your child says he doesn't want to be left with his babysitter, despite being fine yesterday.**

HE SAYS
—
"Don't like her."

YOU MIGHT THINK
—
"Why is he being so rude to the babysitter? It's embarrassing."

Assuming his babysitter is kind and competent, this comment most likely reflects his wish to be with you and his difficulty with transitions, not an actual dislike of the sitter. He doesn't realize that his comment is hurtful. He's just telling you, "I don't like this!"

You might worry that the sitter will feel hurt or quit because of his remark. If you have to be somewhere, you probably feel frustrated at his resistance. You might also wonder if there's a reason for his dislike.

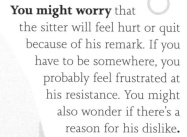

" "

A CARING BABYSITTER OFFERS EXTRA FUN FOR YOUR CHILD AND NEEDED SUPPORT OR A HELPFUL BREAK FOR YOU.

WHAT HE'S THINKING

"I don't want Mommy or Daddy to leave. I want them to stay!"

Many children this age experience bouts of separation anxiety, especially if there are changes at home. Your child wants control over his world, and he loves being with you, so of course he wants you to stay. Also, he doesn't understand time, so if you leave, he's not sure when you'll return. Eventually he'll learn that you always come back.

SEE RELATED TOPICS
Mommy, don't go!: pp.52–53
I want a cuddle: pp.90–91

HOW TO RESPOND

In the moment...

Ease him through the transition. Say, "I'll miss you, too." Explain where you are going and when you'll be back, using concrete events such as "after lunch" or "before naptime." Help him plan what fun activities he can do while he's waiting for you.

Don't drag out goodbye. If your child sees you hesitating to leave him, he'll think that you're not sure he's safe with the sitter. Create a brief goodbye routine, such as giving one hug and blowing two kisses from the door, and calmly use it every time.

Ask the sitter to call, text, or send you a photo once he settles. Most likely, he'll calm down shortly after you leave. You'll feel relieved knowing that his upset didn't last long and he's having fun while you're apart.

In the long term...

Choose a caregiver you trust. In order to be able to confidently leave your child with someone else, you need to know that he's in good hands. Check references and ask questions to get to know the babysitter and how she interacts with children.

Work together with the caregiver to figure out ways to help your child feel comfortable with her. For instance, you may want to start by letting him get used to playing with the sitter while you're nearby. You child might find it easier to handle short separations or having the sitter take him to the park or watch him at your house. You could also suggest a favorite activity the sitter can do with him to help him calm down after you leave.

Shyness

Shy children generally come into the world with more sensitive temperaments. These children may be slower to warm up when meeting new people, but over time they can learn how to get used to unfamiliar situations.

Research shows that about one out of every five babies is highly reactive or easily overwhelmed by new experiences. This can set the stage for later shyness or anxiety. But these inborn, temperamental tendencies aren't destiny. More than half of babies who are very reactive at 4 months are not particularly inhibited with unfamiliar peers at 4½ years of age.

Your child's experiences will soften or reinforce her inborn tendencies. If you overprotect her, she won't learn to manage her fears. If you gently encourage her to try new things and interact with peers, she'll learn to move past her tendency to avoid the unfamiliar.

Your shy child may never become a life-of-the-party extrovert, but she can still build satisfying friendships. There's definitely need in the world for a quieter social style and people who listen more than they talk.

1
Avoid the label.
If your child hides behind you when you go into a new situation, don't excuse her as "shy" to others. Labeling her as such will sound like it's a negative fixed character trait.

4
Normalize her feelings.
Tell her it's normal to feel self-conscious or uncomfortable in a new situation. Encourage her to say hi to just one person, smile and nod while listening to a conversation, or look around and see what other kids are doing then do the same. Explain that her worries will ease as she starts intereracting.

6
Tune into body language.
Explain that we communicate without saying a word. Show her how crossed arms, hunching, frowning, and looking away seem unfriendly, whereas the opposite behaviors seem friendly.

Age by age

2–3
YEARS OLD

Be a secure base
At this stage, introduce your child from the safety of your arms (or your lap) so she can observe and get used to her surroundings first.

Watch together
Hold your child and describe what you see other kids doing. Encourage her to do the same thing near them to ease her into parallel play.

4–5
YEARS OLD

Practice sessions
It's often easier for children to play with kids who are a bit older or younger. They follow the lead of older kids and feel less scared of younger ones. Either can help build social confidence.

Set up playdates
Your child is likely to feel more confident and outgoing with other children in her home territory.

6–7
YEARS OLD

Nudge, don't push
Encourage your child to expand her social world, but don't try to force her to be someone she's not. Value her social strengths, such as loyalty and kindness.

Follow her passions
Look for after-school activities that fit her interests so she can join by doing.

↓

GOOD PRACTICE

8 key principles

2
Reframe shyness.
When first meeting your child, other adults may label her shy to explain why she is not friendly. Head off this description by saying she likes to take her time observing new situations first.

3
Prepare her.
Your child's worries about new situations, such as parties or starting school, will be eased if she knows what to expect. Before she goes, explain what she will see, hear, and do, who will be there, and what to do if she needs help.

5
Teach friendly greetings.
Ease that first moment of contact by helping her learn to look people in the eye (or between their eyebrows, if eye contact feels too difficult), smile, say hi, and tell her name. A friendly greeting says, "I'm happy to see you!"

7
Role-play.
Shy children are particularly worried about saying or doing the wrong thing. Help your child feel more confident by role-playing games with her toys about meeting new people at school or going to a birthday party.

8
Model friendliness.
Children learn more from what we do than from what we say. Let her watch you being friendly to new people, chatting with neighbors and other parents, and spending time with your own friends.

"Let's pretend..."

By the age of 2, pretend play is a key part of your child's development. It allows him to show his curiosity, solve problems, comprehend people and their actions, and improve his social skills. If your child invites you into his make-believe world, accept and follow his lead.

SCENARIO | Your child says he wants to play coffee shop with you.

HE SAYS

"Let's pretend..."

YOU MIGHT THINK

"Again? I think this is the 100th time we've played coffee shop."

In your child's mind, he's taking on the persona of coffee shop owner. He'll relish being in charge and directing you to be a character, playing by his rules. In doing so, he is improving his emerging social skills and boosting his cognitive development by using information from the world around him.

While children love to play make-believe, such games can feel repetitive to many adults. But if your child asks you to take part, join in and be patient. The more you embrace these opportunities of engaging with your child, the more you get to know him and the more fun you can have together.

PRETEND PLAY ALLOWS CHILDREN TO LEARN SKILLS THEY CAN TRANSFER TO THE REAL WORLD—MAKING FRIENDS, PROBLEM-SOLVING, AND SELF-EXPRESSION.

WHAT HE'S THINKING

"I love playing and pretending with you!"

Joining in a game that your toddler has dreamed up will make him feel loved and valued. Because every aspect of the coffee shop is real to him, there's also a delicious sense of power for him in pretend play because he gets to be in charge.

HOW TO RESPOND

In the moment...

Be present. Put all thoughts of other jobs out of your mind and leave your phone in another room. It's worth devoting this short time—say, 10–15 minutes—because of the benefits for your child.

Let him make the rules. If you give your child control over his make-believe world, his need for power is met, and he is less likely to want to take charge in other areas of life. Pretend play allows him to explore ideas, feelings, and relationships. It can help him process experiences and figure out his world.

Wind it down. Instead of abruptly saying the game is over, guide your child toward a wrap-up event or activity. Use language that suits the game: "We'll need to stop after this next customer." If he gets upset, assure him that you can play the game—and open up the coffee shop—again tomorrow.

In the long term...

Make it possible. Set up places around your home with props for role-playing games—a toy stove, a basket of toy fruits and veggies, a doctor's kit, and dress-up items. Take your lead from him; you don't have to join in every time he asks, but do play along at least once a day.

Go with the flow. Don't try to control the game or interrupt your child's flow—or he will think that you're taking over. When a young child is role-playing, he is choosing to work through the experiences that are most important to him—such as mealtimes or talking on the phone. Follow his lead, and don't turn it into a lesson.

SEE RELATED TOPICS
Want this story: pp.76–77
What does this one do?: pp.80–81

"I want it now!"

Being able to to wait is a difficult skill for children to learn. They have to rein in the urgency of their wanting, accept the delay, and trust that they'll get what they want later. Your child will find it easier to wait if you teach her how.

SCENARIO | **When you get a tub of ice cream out of the freezer, you tell your child it will be 5 minutes until it's ready to serve.**

SHE SAYS

"I want it now!"

The more your child wants something, the harder it is for her to wait. Waiting takes executive functioning skills—or thinking and planning in the higher parts of her brain—which are still developing. Children start to be able to think beyond the now between the ages of 3 and 5, but most of us continue to work on cultivating patience well into adulthood.

TEACHING CHILDREN HOW TO WAIT HELPS THEM COPE WITH UNAVOIDABLE DELAYS.

SEE RELATED TOPICS

Blue cup. No, yellow cup. No, blue cup: pp.46–47
No coloring on the wall: pp.174–175

YOU MIGHT THINK

"Her yelling won't make the ice cream soften any faster."

You might be annoyed when your child demands something right now, especially when it's just not possible to give it to her yet. But it makes no sense to get impatient with her for being impatient. Instead, work with her to help her learn to tolerate the delay.

WHAT SHE'S THINKING

"The ice cream's right there. Why can't I eat it now?"

Your child loves ice cream, so she wants it as soon as she sees it. She also thinks you can do anything, so she doesn't understand why you can't instantly make it thawed enough to scoop. The delay makes no sense to her and feels unbearable.

HOW TO RESPOND

In the moment...

Sidetrack her. Toddlers are easily distracted, so shift her attention away from the cause of her frustration—point out something else interesting, such as what the cat's up to in the yard or remind her about a new toy.

Make the time real. If the ice cream needs 5 minutes to soften, set a timer and give her a challenge—for example, how many LEGO pieces can she pick up before the buzzer goes off? When the timer goes off, it's ready to eat. This gives her a more concrete understanding of how long she needs to wait as well as some control over the process.

Keep it out of sight to keep it out of mind. Children find it easier to wait for something if it's out of sight. Put the thawing ice cream somewhere your child can't see it.

In the long term...

Suggest strategies to use while she's waiting. Singing songs, looking at books, drawing, or playing with a toy will make it easier for her to be patient.

Talk about patience. Congratulate her when she manages to wait patiently. Point out the reward that comes after the wait. Tell her, "You did it! You waited calmly in the line for the fairground ride, and now it's your turn!"

"I'm not finished."

At this age, children live in the moment, unconcerned with time, schedules, and adult agendas. If they are enjoying an activity or are absorbed in a game, they can find it frustrating to stop and switch attention to something else, especially if they don't want to do it as much.

SCENARIO | **Your child is playing in the sandbox at the playground. It's time to leave to pick up your older child from school.**

HE SAYS

"I'm not finished."

YOU MIGHT THINK

"Why does he make such a fuss? He knows I've got to pick up his big brother."

While adults have things to do and places to be, children just want to play. It's frustrating for your child to give up his fun for something else. At this age, he can usually focus on only one activity at a time for up to 10–15 minutes—so-called "play islands." So the best time to get him to leave his activity is at the junction of one game and another.

You know school pickup happens at a certain time every weekday, but he's living in the moment and doesn't think about anything but his play. If he seems to drag his feet when you need to be somewhere, you may well feel frustrated.

DEALING WITH TRANSITIONS IS A CRUCIAL ABILITY FOR STARTING SCHOOL. TEACH YOUR CHILD WAYS HE CAN PREPARE FOR CHANGE WHILE HE IS YOUNG.

WHAT HE'S THINKING

"I'm having fun, and I don't want to stop!"

With his growing independence, he wants to be in charge of his playtime. It takes a lot of brain power and self-control for him to stop what he is doing for a reason that is important to you but not to him.

HOW TO RESPOND

In the moment...

Name your child's feelings. Rather than handing out orders, show him you understand. Tell him: "You're having a fun time and are frustrated that we have to go now." When you acknowledge his feelings, he'll feel less need to protest.

Move toward the transition. Instead of asking him to stop instantly, guide him toward a final task. Say, "Make one more sandcastle, and then we have to go." A final task is easier to understand than "5 more minutes."

Make the next activity interesting. If you are asking him to do something he doesn't want to do, such as sit in the back of the car to go to school, suggest singing a song or playing a guessing game in the car on the way.

In the long term...

Give him a job. Let your child help you set a timer on your phone and tell you when it's time to go. Being "in charge" of a transition makes him feel important and more likely to accept the shift.

Become predictable. Making these transitions is harder when your child is tired and hungry. Establishing a routine that revolves around him for meals, naps, and trips to the playground will help make such transitions predictable and easier for him to cope with.

SEE RELATED TOPICS

I want more!: pp.58–59
Let's pretend...: pp.64–65

"Please, please, please."

Now that your child is able to speak, she can express her wishes in words. She will use her newfound ability to ask you for what she wants because she sees you as an all-powerful grown-up who is the source for fulfilling her wishes.

SCENARIO | **In the park, your child spots an ice-cream cart and starts asking repeatedly for ice cream.**

" "

ACCEPTING "NO" IS CHALLENGING FOR YOUNG CHILDREN.

SHE SAYS

"Please, please, please."

At this age, your child knows what she wants and that you often get it for her. She's even figured out that you're more likely to say yes if she asks with a please. She keeps repeating herself because she doesn't know how else to get what she wants and because sometimes nagging and whining work.

SEE RELATED TOPICS
I want more!: pp.58–59
I want it now!: pp.66–67

YOU MIGHT THINK

"Her whining is annoying! Why can't she just accept a simple no?"

WHAT SHE'S THINKING

"I want ice cream now. I really, really want it! I still want it."

Being asked for a treat every time you go out, and being badgered after you've said no, is annoying. You may be tempted to give in to your child's request, just to stop the whining or prevent a tantrum. Unfortunately, that will teach your child that whining is a good way to get what she wants.

At this stage, children engage in "wishful thinking." They believe just wanting something means they can get it. Your child also thinks that if she keeps asking, you'll eventually say yes. Her focus is on her wanting, not your frustration.

HOW TO RESPOND

In the moment...

Show her you've heard. Acknowledge her wish. Say, "You sure love ice cream!" or "That would be yummy."

You decide. As an adult, you can see beyond the present moment. Say no, gently but firmly, if that's the wise choice, even if she protests.

Explain why. She'll still be disappointed, but a no is easier to accept if she understands the reasons behind it.

Stay calm. You don't have to get angry or be harsh to say no and mean it. Acknowledge her disappointment. Distract her or say what she can do instead. If necessary, stop talking and just wait out her upset.

In the long term...

Plan ahead. If you know you won't be able to do something your child wants or expects, warning her beforehand can help her cope. Role-play, at a neutral time, to help her practice polite requests and accepting no.

"Not Mommy. Want Daddy."

Now that your toddler is no longer a baby and can express his desires more clearly, he is seeking more control over some aspects of his life. One of the ways he may try to do this is by choosing which parent he does different activities with.

SCENARIO | Despite you offering to role-play pirates, your child wants to play only with Daddy; Mommy won't do.

HE SAYS

"Not Mommy. Want Daddy."

Assigning roles to parents is one way that children try to exercise control and make their world predictable. Right now, he's insisting that playing pirates is a Daddy activity, but he might also insist that only Mommy can read him stories or brush his teeth.

YOU MIGHT THINK

"Does this mean he doesn't love me as much as Daddy?"

It can hurt to hear your child say he'd rather do something with his other parent. You may even feel jealous or resentful of your partner. However, this is a short-lived phase, so try not to take his words personally. He doesn't mean to reject. He just wants to decide who does what.

SEE RELATED TOPICS

Mommy, don't go!: pp.52–53
I like this stick: pp.78–79

WHAT HE'S THINKING

"I love Mommy, but I'm craving Daddy right now."

There are many reasons why your child may ask for his other parent. His choice might express a wish for sameness or for variety. It might also reflect your different personalities or styles of relating. For example, studies show that fathers are more likely to take part in rough-and-tumble play.

HOW TO RESPOND

In the moment...

Allow him some choice. If you can easily go along with your child's wishes, and you don't mind doing so, go ahead. But it's also fine to say, "I know you like having Daddy do that, but tonight it's Mommy's turn."

Join the fun. You don't have to stand on the sidelines. Acknowledge his feelings and join in. Say something like, "You sure love playing with Daddy. Me, too! Let's all play!"

In the long term...

Develop your connection. If you think your child may be asking for his other parent because he has more fun with him, set aside daily one-on-one time to develop fun activities you can do together, too.

Be a team. Children feel safest when they have a team of adult carers working together to look after them. Show your child that you and Daddy can both meet his needs. Team members don't necessarily have to do things exactly the same way, so embrace your own style of caring for your child.

Talk to your partner. Let your partner know how you feel so resentment doesn't build up between you. Avoid making critical comments in front of your child, and set aside more time together as a family.

Sleep difficulties

All parents know that children are happier and better behaved when they are well rested. However, that doesn't mean that children welcome going to bed— or that they will stay in bed throughout the night.

Children can have two main types of sleep problems: not wanting to go to bed in the first place and waking up during the night.

Some children don't want to go to sleep because being alone in the dark seems scary. Their imaginations conjure up monsters or burglars. Others have busy minds and find it hard to transition to a more relaxed state. Still others just don't want to miss out when parents or older siblings stay up later.

Children have more periods of light sleep than adults, which can contribute to night-time problems. Bad dreams or night terrors can also complicate things.

Getting a child into a sleep routine is one of the hardest parenting challenges. But when you achieve it, it can make one of the most positive differences to family life. See your role as helping your child develop a healthy attitude toward sleep and enjoy time in her bed.

1
Set the stage for sleep.
Wake her up at the same time every day. Make sure her bed and room are comfortable. Let her run around during the day so she's tired but head for bed before she's overtired and wired.

4
Make bedtime special.
Never threaten to send your child to bed as a punishment. Portray bedtime as a special time to snuggle up with a book before she gets the rest she needs to grow well, learn, and have lots of energy.

7
Keep it calm and unrushed.
To help soothe your child's active brain, turn off screens an hour before bed. Speak softly and allow up to an hour from starting bath to lights out.

9
Keep it low key.
After lights out, help meet any need for a drink, a toilet visit, or a quick hug for reassurance, but try to engage as little as possible so fussing is not rewarded with your attention.

GOOD PRACTICE
10 key principles

2
Create a plan.
Consistency is key, so work out a plan that you and your family can stick to. Decide on one change at a time, such as getting your child to bed without a fight or getting her to stay in bed all night. Changes can take up to two weeks.

3
Present a united front.
Disagreements over how and when to get children into bed can cause tension between partners who lose out on precious adult time. If your child gets mixed messages, she may try to play you off against one other.

5
Tell your child what she is doing right.
Notice and describe what she does right as she gets ready for bed. Consider offering extra privileges, such as a special breakfast or an extra game to celebrate a peaceful night.

6
Create sleep cues.
Nighttime routines are full of signals associated with falling asleep. As adults, we take these cues for granted—getting undressed, brushing teeth, and reading a book in bed. Create these cues for your child by doing the steps in the same order every night.

8
Get a night-light.
Young children can feel as if the darkness hides all the familiar objects in their bedroom. A dim nightlight can show them nothing has changed and doesn't interrupt their sleep.

10
Ease into new routines.
If your child is used to falling asleep with you in her room, help her gain the confidence to sleep on her own by gradually moving farther away or agreeing to check on her every 5 minutes if she lies quietly in her bed.

! TAILORED ADVICE
Age by age

2–3
YEARS OLD

Snooze, don't lose
Your child needs about 12–13 hours of sleep at this stage. So make sure she gets to bed at the right time.

Get a sleep buddy
Studies show that having a stuffed animal to protect them or who needs their comfort at night helps kids sleep.

4–5
YEARS OLD

Scrap the nap
By now, your child may need less sleep, so you may want to cut out daytime naps.

Nightmares or night terrors
If your child has a nightmare, distract her with a pleasant thought or change the story so it's silly and let the scary images fade. To prevent night terrors, try waking your child 15–30 minutes before they usually occur.

6–7
YEARS OLD

Can't fall asleep?
Tell your child sleep is like peeing—eventually her body will do what it needs to do. She just needs to rest, lying quietly with her eyes closed and thinking happy thoughts.

Handle worries
Friendship or school worries can keep your child up. Pick a time—well before bedtime—when she can talk things through with you.

"Want this story."

Sharing books helps children learn to speak, interact, improve their attention span, and read sooner themselves. When part of a routine, story time also helps to signal that it's time for sleep. Such undivided attention will make your child feel safe, special, and connected to you.

SCENARIO | Your child wants you to read that story—again—at bedtime.

HE SAYS

"Want this story."

YOU MIGHT THINK

"I've read this book 100 times. Why does he keep choosing it?"

Sharing a story is a calm and relaxing way for your child to wind down. Beyond giving him a cue to sleep, story time comes with many benefits; children who are read to frequently at ages 2 or 3 do better academically once they start school.

You probably know many books by heart, because your child wants to hear his favorites again and again. While the lack of variety can be frustrating for you, hearing a familiar story gives him a sense of security and helps develop his memory, vocabulary, and word recognition.

"

READING STORIES IS A PRECIOUS OPPORTUNITY TO BOND, RELAX, HAVE FUN, AND HELP YOUR CHILD LEARN ALL AT THE SAME TIME.

WHAT HE'S THINKING

"Can we read it again? It makes me feel so good."

A current favorite book may express an interest, wish, situation, idea, or concern your child is pondering. Your conversation about the book deepens his understanding. Once your child masters the themes in a story, he's likely to move on to a new favorite book.

HOW TO RESPOND

In the moment...

Give your child your full attention. Let your child relax knowing this is time for the two of you and he is your priority now. Put phones out of sight.

Ask and answer questions. Continuous interruptions can be frustrating for adults, but your child's questions are key to helping him interact with the story and stretch his imagination. Ask what he thinks will happen next, and talk about the characters' feelings to encourage the emotional understanding needed for friendships.

Use lots of expression. Bring stories to life by giving characters different voices to match their personalities. Trying out various voices and volumes can help your child understand the meaning of new words. The more he enjoys the story, the more he is likely to learn from it.

In the long term...

Agree on the number of books upfront. If your child often asks you to read half of his bookshelf, suggest that he chooses three books every night at the start of story time and stick to those.

Make it a ritual. Read him at least one book at bedtime as well as stories during the day, if that's possible. They don't have to be long. Even if you are tired, it's important for him to have peaceful, calm, one-on-one time with you in the evenings, which makes him feel secure.

◀ SEE RELATED TOPICS ▶
Let's pretend...: pp.64–65
Carving out quality time: pp.84–85

"I like this stick."

When you pushed your child in a stroller, you knew roughly how long it would take to get from A to B. But now your child is walking by herself, and it feels like it can take ages to get anywhere because she is fascinated by so much of what she sees.

SCENARIO | **On the way to a playgroup, your child insists on stopping to inspect yet another interesting stick.**

THIS IS A UNIQUE TIME OF EXPLORATION FOR YOUR CHILD. ADAPT YOUR PACE TO FIT IN WITH HERS.

SHE SAYS

"I like this stick."

Your child is thrilled with her growing ability to explore the outside world independently. She loves being able to stop and look instead of whizzing by in a stroller, so every few steps she finds something new to fascinate her. She's curious about the texture, color, and weight of her discoveries.

SEE RELATED TOPICS

I'm not finished: pp.68–69
What does this one do?: pp.80–81

YOU MIGHT THINK

"I love her curiosity, but this is taking forever! We're late now."

WHAT SHE'S THINKING

"This stick is so interesting!"

If you need to be somewhere at a specific time, it's easy to get frustrated when the journey progresses slowly. Urging her to hurry won't help. Her lack of time awareness, intense focus, and ability to think about only one thing at a time make it hard for her to move along.

Your child is building connections between her brain cells at a speed of 1,000 a second. She's programmed to make the most of this rapid cognitive development stage by noticing everything. She is living "in the moment," and it takes a lot of brain power to switch from her agenda to yours.

HOW TO RESPOND

In the moment...

Get down to her level. Crouch down to let her show you what she's found. When you need to get going, draw her attention to something farther along the path to encourage her to move along.

Relish the journey. Children understand living in the present, but adults usually need to practice this. As your child explores, try mindfully walking with her. Walk slowly, noticing everything you can, through all your senses, without judgment.

In the long term...

Build in buffer time. The more time pressure you put on yourself to get to places, the more difficult it will be to step into your child's world. Children learn best when they are not hurried and can follow their own interests.

Let her collect treasures. Young children enjoy bringing home mementos from their wanderings. Choose an outdoor spot near your home where your child can put the sticks, stones, and flowers she collects.

Prioritize time outside. Spending time outdoors gives children the chance to run, jump, climb, and explore nature. It's also linked to better mood.

"What does this one do?"

Children are natural scientists. They want to explore, experiment, and discover how the world works. The more inquisitive a child is, the more he learns. Parents can encourage children's curiosity and eagerness to learn with lifelong benefits.

SCENARIO | After seeing you take some photos, your child wants to play with your camera to learn how it works.

HE SAYS

"What does this one do?"

YOU MIGHT THINK

"Uh oh. If he fiddles with everything, he's going to lose my settings."

At this age, your child loves hands-on learning. He prods and pokes, eagerly exploring his ability to make things happen. Pressing the buttons in an elevator, stepping on the mat in front of an automatic door, or (oops!) turning off the lights in a public building are thrilling experiences for him.

Because your child is always twiddling knobs and pushing buttons, you may feel you can't take your eyes off him for a second. Redirect him if you need to, but welcome his curiosity, so he feels safe and encouraged in his quest for answers.

SEE RELATED TOPICS
Want your phone: pp.56–57
When is tomorrow?: pp.86–87

> ## YOUR ENCOURAGEMENT IS A KEY FACTOR IN KEEPING THE DRIVE TO LEARN STRONG.

WHAT HE'S THINKING

"This makes a great noise. And I want to see how this part works."

Your child is fascinated by cause and effect—he loves the fact that he can press a button to make something happen—just like a jack-in-the box. This gives him a sense of control over his world and helps him learn how to anticipate events.

HOW TO RESPOND

In the moment...

Describe what the buttons do. By explaining what each button does in simple words, you add to your child's understanding, which he can build on to find out more.

Ask him questions. Ask your child what he sees or hears, what he predicts will happen, and how he thinks things work. This deepens his understanding by integrating what he learns with what he already knows.

Work on the answer together. When you're not sure of the answer, encourage his curiosity by saying, "Good question. Let's find out. I want to know, too."

In the long term...

Model curiosity. Let your child see you learning new things by reading books, trying new recipes, visiting museums, or exploring a hobby.

Be patient. Be prepared to answer long lists of questions and even the same question more than once. Your child may ask again because he forgot, he wants to see if you'll answer the same way, or he just likes chatting with you. Studies find that, by age 7, children ask substantially fewer questions if they are not encouraged. Your patient responses keep his curiosity alive.

"One for you, one for me."

Learning to share is an important skill, which has to be taught to all children. It's good to model sharing as much as possible so children will do the same with their peers. Being able to share is a key factor in helping them make and keep friends.

SCENARIO | **Your child is making a show of sharing her cookies—even though you don't really want any.**

SHE SAYS

"One for you, one for me."

YOU MIGHT THINK

"I really don't want a well-handled cookie."

As your child gained more control over her body, first she learned she had the ability to grab things and wanted to keep everything to herself. Now, she's reaching a new milestone—developing the empathy to realize that others have wants, too, while also mastering her impulses to hog it all.

All parents want their children to be good sharers, because they want them to be seen as kind and to be liked by others. But you may have to wait until your child is about 3 before she understands she makes others happy by sharing. Until that time, encourage and reinforce her sharing offers.

◄ SEE RELATED TOPICS ►

That's mine!: pp.36–37
Let's pretend…: pp.64–65

SHARING HAS TO BE TAUGHT, SO SHOW YOUR CHILD HOW TO DO IT. IT IS A CENTRAL SKILL FOR FRIENDSHIPS.

WHAT SHE'S THINKING

"I like this rule. It makes me feel good and makes Mommy happy."

Children love to repeat things they enjoy, and your child is no exception. The more she repeats such rituals with you, the more she's learning how to share—an important skill for her future.

HOW TO RESPOND

In the moment...

Smile and take the cookie. Reinforce the message that sharing is good, by encouraging sharing with your child and others as much as you can.

Thank her. Let her know that you're grateful for her fairness and generosity; you can always say you're saving your cookie for later.

In the long term...

Describe her impact on others. Caring for others motivates sharing. Help your child see the effects of her kindness. For example, "Did you see how Laura smiled when you gave her a cookie? She really liked that."

Start with taking turns. It's easier for children to share when it's temporary. Teach your child to count or sing a song while waiting to manage taking turns with siblings. Board games can also help her practice taking turns.

Dont insist that she share her most precious possessions. New gifts and toys can be just hers.

Carving out quality time

However busy life gets, it's important to set aside a period most days to give your child undivided love and attention. Such regular one-on-one times are likely to be the most special moments for both of you.

Your relationship with your child is shaped by the time you spend together. The most important thing is to be responsive: when your child is seeking your attention, try to turn toward him more often than away.

Although you can't create more hours in the day, you can prioritize setting aside some special time in what you do have. Be reassured that all your efforts will be rewarded. Such together times are when your child feels closest to you—and some of your best memories are made.

Finding ways to regularly spend some time focusing only on your child can build a sense of closeness and may even decrease negative attention-seeking behavior, such as whining and arguing. Over time, even brief periods of regular, one-on-one, special time can make a big difference.

1

Set aside 10–15 minutes. Aim for short chunks daily with each child and be consistent. Your child will look forward to this time and so will you.

4

Make the most of vacations. In addition to recharging batteries, vacations are key bonding times. Really connect with your child by creating opportunities to genuinely enjoy each other's company.

6

Find the best time of day. You might want to start the day sitting on your child's bed, stroking his hair, and chatting; play together while the baby is napping; or have some extra snuggling before bed. Find what works best for your family.

GOOD PRACTICE
8 key principles

2
Label it.
It's key that your child understands that you have set aside this time to be with him. At the start, tell him it's your "special time" together.

3
Focus on the freebies.
Spend time with your child on activities that don't cost money. There's so much you can do—playing card games, cooking, taking family walks or bike rides, and walking the dog—to show that just being together is enough.

5
Maximize every opportunity.
Whenever you're with just one child—driving or running errands—use that time to connect. Touching, chatting, doing things together…these are all ways to show your child that you're glad to be with him.

7
Have fun together.
Fun activities release feel-good neurochemicals and contribute to positive relationships.

8
Turn off the technology.
Put away your phone during special time. Try to clear your mind so you can stay present with your child.

" "
SETTING ASIDE EVEN A SHORT AMOUNT OF "SPECIAL TIME" DAILY SUPPORTS AND DEEPENS YOUR BOND.

"When is tomorrow?"

Adults think a lot about time, whether it's minutes and hours or yesterday, today, and tomorrow. Young children understand only what they can touch or feel; time is an abstract concept, and they need help to understand when things are going to happen.

SCENARIO | **Your child knows her grandparents are visiting tomorrow, but she keeps asking where they are.**

SHE SAYS

"When is tomorrow?"

> **YOUNG CHILDREN ARE NOT BEING UNREASONABLE WHEN THEY SHOW IMPATIENCE. THEY CANNOT YET SEE HOW TIME PASSES.**

Your child lives mainly in the moment. Her concept of the passage of time is based on knowing that things happen regularly—getting up, eating meals, and going to bed. By hearing you link happenings to words, such as "first," "next," "now," "then," "before," and "after," she will begin to grasp the idea of time as a sequence. But "tomorrow" is still too far away for her to imagine.

◆ SEE RELATED TOPICS ▶
Want your phone: pp.56–57
I want it now: pp.66–67

YOU MIGHT THINK

"I've told her they're coming tomorrow. Why does she keep asking when they'll arrive?"

WHAT SHE'S THINKING

"I want my grandparents to come now."

Toddlers think mainly in terms of "now" and "not now." Tomorrow is "not now," and she has no idea when it will arrive. You can help her understand by putting future events in context. For example, tell her, "We will eat dinner, then go to bed, then they will be here for breakfast."

Waiting is hard, even for adults. Minutes can feel like hours when we're eager for something to happen. Your warm understanding of her excitement and frustration about the delay in seeing her grandparents will help her cope.

HOW TO RESPOND

In the moment...

Acknowledge feelings. Say, "You're excited to see them!" or "You wish they were here already!" to express empathy and help your child understand and manage her feelings.

Distract her. Waiting will be easier to tolerate if your child is busy with fun activities.

In the long term...

Ask what's next. Have a predictable bedtime routine, such as brush teeth, read story, kiss goodnight. See if your child can tell you what comes next in the routine to help her understand a simple sequence.

Plan the week. Create a visual calendar for the week so your child can begin to understand that certain things happen on certain days. For instance, you can explain that Monday and Wednesday are school days.

Make it visual. Use simple pictures of routine events, such as meals, day care, or bedtime, to show your child how long it is until Grandma and Grandpa arrive. Let her cross out each event after it happens, so she can see she's getting closer to the big event.

CHAPTER 4

4–5
YEARS OLD

"I want a cuddle."

At this age, your child is programmed to be attached and stay close to the person he spends the most time with and who makes him feel the most safe. Even when children start to strike out on their own, they still need the security of an adult and a comforting cuddle.

SCENARIO | **Your child won't leave your arms to join in a friend's birthday party.**

HE SAYS

"I want a cuddle."

YOU MIGHT THINK

"He normally can't wait to go off and explore. Why is he being so clingy today?"

Despite your child knowing most of the children at this party, when you arrive, the novelty and noise may be overwhelming. He may need reassurance and security from you. He may be thinking: "Help! This is new and scary to me."

Acknowledge that this behavior, though surprising, is a sign that he trusts you to comfort him—your child can signal that he still wants you to keep him safe in this unfamiliar place. Ask yourself whether he's ready to be this independent. Enjoy the cuddles while he plucks up the courage to join in.

INTRODUCE HIM TO OTHERS FROM THE SAFETY OF YOUR ARMS SO HE CAN OBSERVE HIS SURROUNDINGS AND GET USED TO THEM FIRST.

WHAT HE'S THINKING

"Mom, don't let go. I need some extra comfort before I can join in."

Research has found that 10 to 20 percent of children come into the world wired with slightly more vigilant nervous systems, which makes them more cautious in new situations. It doesn't mean your child won't make friends. He just needs you a little longer as his secure base.

HOW TO RESPOND

In the moment...

Don't force him to join in. Do cuddle and keep him close. And avoid saying he's a big boy now and he must run along and play. Give him time to adjust to the situation.

Get him noticing what's going on. Keep him focused outward by pointing out what's going on, whether it's the birthday cake on the table or a friendly party game in progress. Something will catch his eye that will make it hard for him to resist joining in.

Don't label him as "shy." Acknowledge his feelings—that he's unsure about the party because it is crowded—but avoid referring to him as shy, or he will feel permanently branded as such. Cuddle him without question or judgment.

Praise his bravery. When he does start to look around and show an interest in joining in, give him targeted praise. Tell him you know it's tricky, but he's done really well and is brave to join in.

In the long term...

Practice social situations. Take your child with you when you go out so he gets practice meeting others in smaller groups and quieter places. Your child needs to be in social situations to learn how to be social. Let him see you being outgoing and happy to meet people, too, at parties or at school and neighborhood events.

SEE RELATED TOPICS
Shyness: pp.62–63
I want my pacifier: pp.94–95

"Look what I did!"

Your 4- or 5-year-old will be very clear about wanting you to take notice of her and what she does. We all have a fundamental psychological need for recognition, but children especially need lots of positive attention for healthy cognitive and emotional development.

SCENARIO | Your child has just finished her favorite puzzle.

SHE SAYS

"Look what I did!"

YOU MIGHT THINK

"I have so much to do. Why does she want me to see that again?"

She is desperate for you to come over and look at it immediately. We are programmed from birth to need recognition and be acknowledged by others. This is one of the key building blocks of self-worth.

Whether or not your child has achieved something new is irrelevant—she can't help but crave your recognition. Interruptions can be irksome, but if you show that you're angry or irritated, then she might seek attention instead by misbehaving. Your loving attention is what's needed now.

"

YOUR ATTENTION, PRAISE, AND UNCONDITIONAL LOVE ARE THE BIGGEST INFLUENCES ON YOUR CHILD.

WHAT SHE'S THINKING

"Your approval is really important to me!"

Not only does your child want your attention, but she also needs your social approval. Children have a built-in radar to detect praise that doesn't sound genuine or intended. She'll process any lack of sincerity or distraction (being glued to your phone, for instance) as rejection

SEE RELATED TOPICS

You're always too busy: pp.128–129
You promised: pp.168–169

HOW TO RESPOND

In the moment...

Manage unavoidable delays. If you can't stop immediately to respond to your child, maybe because you're making dinner or on an important call, tell her "I'll come as soon as I've…" and then keep your word. You may want to suggest something she can do while she's waiting for you to finish.

Notice what she's done right. Instead of just reeling off another "Good job," take a moment to notice what she's done and refer to something specific: "I really like the colors in that jigsaw" or "What a fun picture."

Show unsolicited approval from time to time. Offer encouraging words even when she isn't asking for it directly—for example, if you notice her playing well or being cooperative. Frequent bursts of attention and comments during the day will help build her confidence and self-belief as well as discover exactly what sort of behavior you want to see.

In the long term...

Avoid delaying tactics. "I'm busy; wait a minute." Chances are a minute will turn into several minutes, and the opportunity may pass. Not stopping at that moment means you're repeatedly denying her calls for attention—such an approach can knock her confidence and self-belief.

Make it work for you. You don't always have to sit down and play to give your child positive attention. It's your attention and recognition she wants; she will also love copying you and doing whatever it is you're doing. Enjoy such quality moments.

"I want my pacifier."

Sucking has a powerfully calming effect, which is why many parents give their babies pacifiers to help them soothe themselves. But as they grow older, children can find letting go of this habit hard without lots of encouragement.

SCENARIO | **Your child is ready to start preschool. But he still insists on having his pacifier for most of the day.**

HE SAYS

"I want my pacifier."

You may well have started using a pacifier as a way to help your baby or young child relax and go to sleep, but over time it has become a comfort for him in the daytime, too. He may feel he needs his pacifier to relax, but he just needs to learn other ways of regulating emotions.

" "
YOUR CHILD'S PACIFIER IS OUTLIVING ITS PURPOSE, AND, WITH YOUR HELP, HE IS READY TO FIND NEW WAYS TO RELAX AND SOOTHE HIMSELF.

YOU MIGHT THINK

"He loves his pacifier, but I'm worried it will wreck his teeth."

You probably expected that he would grow out of his need for a pacifier, but some children need extra help setting their pacifier aside and learning other ways to comfort themselves. Dentists recommend limiting pacifier use by age 2 and stopping it by age 4.

SEE RELATED TOPICS
I want a cuddle: pp.90–91
I lost teddy: pp.126–127

"My pacifier makes me feel good. I can't feel better without it."

Your child's brain has created an association between sucking on the pacifier and feeling calm—it's become a habit. He may be upset at first, but if he is encouraged to go without his pacifier for ever-longer periods (with distractions), the habit loop will be broken.

HOW TO RESPOND

In the moment...

Talk to your child. Explain that it's time for the pacifier to go away because he needs his mouth free for talking, eating, and playing. Don't say that you're giving it away to a baby, because your child could feel jealous.

Offer alternatives. Before you take away the pacifier, show your child other ways to feel calm—singing to himself, holding a cuddly toy close, or talking to you.

In the long term...

Wean him off. Start by limiting when he can use a pacifier. For example, you may say he can use it only upstairs and then, later, only in bed. Put it away—out of sight is really out of mind.

Trade it in. Give him some notice, and say at the end of three days he can collect all his pacifiers together and put them in a box to be recycled overnight. Then he'll have a surprise waiting for him the next morning.

Select the time carefully. Choose a stress-free period when you can be around to offer comfort and distraction—a holiday or period of time off work is ideal. Expect it to take up to two weeks for him to stop asking for it. Once it's gone, be careful not to backtrack.

"Are you sad, Mommy?"

As a parent, you're used to responding when your child cries in distress or because she has hurt herself. You may be surprised and touched when she tries to comfort you when you're sad. Discussing your emotions at times with your child can help her develop emotional intelligence.

SCENARIO | After a stressful day, your child finds you in tears.

SHE SAYS

"Are you sad, Mommy?"

Your child now understands that other people can have thoughts and emotions that are different from her own. She's curious about emotions and, because she loves you, wants to comfort you if you're upset—especially if she didn't cause it.

YOU MIGHT THINK

"I don't want her to see me like this. I wish she didn't see me crying."

Your child tends to see you as an all-powerful "superhero" figure, so you may be embarrassed to show your vulnerable side. However, her caring concern is a testament to the empathetic parenting she has received from you. Also, seeing your tears helps her grasp that everyone cries sometimes, and it's not dangerous or shameful.

> **TELL YOUR CHILD THAT CRYING IS A NORMAL AND HEALTHY RESPONSE WHEN PEOPLE FEEL SAD.**

WHAT SHE'S THINKING

"Why is Mommy crying? Did I do something bad?"

It can be scary for children to see their parent feeling very emotional, but it's also a learning opportunity. Talking about what you're feeling, why, and how you'll cope helps your child understand emotions.

HOW TO RESPOND

In the moment...

1

Accept your tears. Crying is a normal, natural reaction to emotional or physical pain. Don't be ashamed of occasionally crying in front of your child. Help her know how to respond by saying, "I could use a hug."

2

Talk through your feelings. Without going into too much detail, explain the core reasons you are sad using "I feel" statements so that she learns to describe her feelings, too. For example, "I feel sad today because I had an argument with my friend."

3

Reassure her. Most of all, children want to know that they are safe and will always be looked after and loved. When your tears have dried, tell her, "I feel better now," and give a smile and a hug. Make it clear that you were not crying because of anything she said or did.

In the long term...

Find the right support. If you're facing a difficult time, make sure you have other caring adults who can offer comfort and support for you. Talking things over with a partner, family member, friend, or mental health professional might help.

Talk about your positive emotions, too. No emotion is bad, but we tend to pay more attention to the negative ones. Talk to your child about times when you feel happy, too. This will help her to notice and appreciate different emotions and to see that life contains a mix of feelings.

SEE RELATED TOPICS

I want a cuddle: pp.90–91
They called me a crybaby: pp.138–139

"I'm so mad!"

Anger is a basic emotion. It occurs, beginning around 1 year of age, when children perceive that they are blocked from reaching some goal. It takes time and practice for children to learn how to manage anger and communicate it effectively.

SCENARIO | **Your child loses his temper after waiting to go on a swing when another child grabs it as it becomes free.**

HE SAYS

"I'm so mad!"

YOU MIGHT THINK

"I get why he's angry, but he can't flip out over every little thing."

Like all emotions, anger is useful. It can give us focus and energy to overcome obstacles or stand up to injustice. But it can also be expressed in unhealthy or hurtful ways. Most children have fewer tantrums as they become more verbal, but some very intense children need extra help learning to cope with anger.

If your child often loses his temper, you may anxiously dread his next outburst. You may also be embarrassed about his outbursts in public and wonder if people judge you for the fact that he hasn't outgrown tantrums or worry that his temper will make other children not want to be his friend.

HELP YOUR CHILD LEARN TO COPE WITH ANGER IN HEALTHY WAYS SO HE CAN AVOID MELTDOWNS—ESPECIALLY IN PUBLIC.

HOW TO RESPOND

In the moment...

Handle it like a tantrum. The first thing to do is help him calm down from his hyper-aroused state. Move him somewhere quiet, where others are not watching him, so he can regain self-control and start to think.

Keep calm. Getting angry with your child for being angry is like throwing gas on a fire. Be present without being intrusive. Speak softly and acknowledge his feelings. "You're mad because she grabbed the swing." Take a walk together, so he can move. Wait until he's calmer to discuss his behavior or coping options.

In the long term...

Give him the words. Teach your child to use "I" statements to explain what he wants or express what he's feeling without resorting to a tantrum. He could say, "I was here first. It's my turn," or "I'm mad that you cut in front of me." Assertive communication is respectful of both the self and others.

Get perspective. Help your child learn to judge the size of a problem. Does it ruin his life forever, or is it a brief frustration? Is he seriously injured or just bothered? Have him use his hands to show the size of various problems you suggest—out of favorite cereal, best friend moves away—so he gets practice judging this. His reaction should match the size of the problem.

Keep your child's tank full. Make sure your child gets plenty of sleep and regular healthy meals and exercise. Without them, he'll be already putting his system under stress and will be more easily triggered.

WHAT HE'S THINKING

"It's not fair that the other child got my turn!"

When children become emotionally flooded, they can't plan, they can't problem solve, they can't understand someone else's perspective... they just can't think. They're at risk for doing something rash or hurtful. Your child needs you to help him settle down. He also needs to learn how to respond to provocation without going nuclear.

SEE RELATED TOPICS
You have to: pp.150–151
It feels nice: pp.162–163

"I'm just going to do it."

All children are naturally impulsive: it takes time and practice to control their actions and not do the first thing that comes into their heads. Be patient while your child learns to apply her "mental brakes" before doing something she knows she shouldn't.

SCENARIO | **You told your child not to start painting until her apron is on, but she starts anyway and gets paint on her clothes.**

SHE SAYS

"I'm just going to do it."

YOU MIGHT THINK

"When I tell her not to do something, why can't she just listen?"

Learning impulse control can be a slow process. It's especially hard for children to rein themselves in when they're excited, scared, or angry. To develop self-control, your child needs guidances from you and plenty of practice.

When you expressly tell a child not to do something, it can be frustrating when she seems to deliberately defy you. She's not trying to be disobedient. Her impulse to act is just stronger than her mental brakes.

" "

CHILDREN ARE NATURALLY IMPULSIVE. HELP THEM TO MAINTAIN THEIR NATURAL CURIOSITY WHILE LEARNING TO LIVE BY RULES.

WHAT SHE'S THINKING

"I'm so excited about painting. I can't wait to get started."

At this age, the thinking-planning part of your child's brain is maturing all the time. This is the "chairperson" in her mind, which has the final say in whether to do something or not. Sometimes, the emotional or physical urge to do something can be so great that it overrules logic or reason, but over time, the "chairperson" will gain more control.

◄ SEE RELATED TOPICS ►
I do it!: pp.38–39
Look what I did!: pp.92–93

HOW TO RESPOND

In the moment...

Redirect. It's easier for your child to listen if you tell her what she should do rather than what she shouldn't. "No," "Stop," and "Don't" are challenging instructions for kids. Instead, turn your no into a yes to work with, rather than against her tendency to act. Tell her "Grab the apron before you start" rather than "Don't start yet."

Have her repeat the instruction. If your child seems distracted, check that she has processed what you've asked her to do by saying, "Please explain to me what I just told you." Also, see whether she can explain the why behind your direction.

In the long term...

Be patient. Some children simply have more impulsive natures and take longer than others to learn self-control. With time, guidance, and practice, your child will learn to manage her impulses.

Set her up for success. Make your home an environment where it's easy for her to make good choices. Put away temptations, find good alternatives to replace past impulsive actions, and stay near her when you know she'll struggle to wait.

Play waiting games. Make practicing self-control fun by playing games that involve putting on the brakes. For instance, dance to music then have your child freeze when you suddenly stop the music. Kids ages 5 and up may enjoy commercial games (such as Hands Down, Snap, or Jenga) that involve taking turns, waiting, and being careful.

"That's so funny!"

Laughing with your child is one of the best ways to feel closer, as well as brighten up family life. A good sense of humor can also make your child happier, more optimistic, and more resilient in the face of the ups and downs of childhood.

SCENARIO | Even while you're doing household chores, your child loves telling you jokes and making you laugh.

HE SAYS

"That's so funny!"

Telling jokes is an important milestone. It means your child is cognitively advanced enough to play with ideas and contrast what's expected with what's unexpected. Having learned what's normal, your child finds jokes funny because they portray the unexpected. A dog that says moo or putting a sock on his ear is hilarious to him.

LAUGHING TOGETHER IS A DELIGHTFUL WAY TO CONNECT WITH YOUR CHILD.

SEE RELATED TOPICS

I love being with you: pp.108–109
When I was little…: pp.114–115

YOU MIGHT THINK

"Oh no, not this one again!"

WHAT HE'S THINKING

"It makes me feel good when I make Daddy laugh."

There will be times when you may tire of your child's more repetitive jokes or the ones where he tells a long story that's just a string of absurdities. Incongruous ideas—such as a chicken crossing the road—are novel for him, and his joke-telling shows he loves interacting with you.

Your child loves the ritual of telling a joke: he says something, you respond, he says something else, and you laugh together. He may go through a stage of telling pre-jokes along the lines of: "Knock, knock!" "Who's there?" "Apple!" "Apple who?" "Apple is wearing a glove!"

HOW TO RESPOND

In the moment...

Respond warmly. Be an appreciative audience of your child's humor attempts. Smile, laugh, and say, "That's funny!" His delight at your reaction will make him want to continue trying to be funny.

Gather material. Humor—if it isn't annoying—can help your child connect with peers. Read joke books together so he can learn new ones to share. Model child-friendly humor. Embrace silly sounds, goofy falls and stunts, and knock-knock jokes. Avoid sarcasm or mockery.

In the long term...

Gloss over toilet humor. At this age, many children find potty talk hilarious. If you respond with disgust or embarrassment, the allure of the forbidden will make these jokes seem even funnier.

Laugh together often. Keep humor at the heart of family life. Be playful about daily routines. Talk with an accent, turn clean-up into a game, make animal noises and chase him. Enjoy funny books and movies together.

Shift gears. Some kids have trouble knowing when it's time to stop being funny and may tip over into being annoying. Gently redirect your child: "That was fun, but silly time is over now. It's time to brush your teeth."

"Can Mr. Giraffe sit down, too?"

Most young children play pretend games and talk to their toy animals or dolls as if they were real. Almost 40 percent take such play further and create an invisible friend. Your child is more likely to do this if she's an only child or there's a big age gap with older siblings.

SCENARIO | Your child insists on setting a place at the table at every meal for her imaginary friend.

SHE SAYS

"Can Mr. Giraffe sit down, too?"

YOU MIGHT THINK

"Is this okay? Is it normal to have an imaginary friend?"

In trying to find areas of life where she can exert power, your child may think it's fun to have made-up friends because she can play what she likes and she can decide what happens next.

You may worry that inventing an imaginary friend means your child is lonely, but it's perfectly normal. Such a friend (whether invisible or a personified object, such as Mr. Giraffe) gives her a chance to stretch her imagination, talk about feelings, work through worries, and exert control.

SEE RELATED TOPICS
I lost teddy: pp.126–127
I didn't do it: pp.142–143

WHAT SHE'S THINKING

"I love playing with him. And I can blame him for the naughty things I do."

Your child knows her friend exists only in her mind. But she'd like to include him as much as possible in the real world—even as an accomplice in mischief!

HOW TO RESPOND

In the moment...

Play along. Never scold your child for making up her friend, but be clear that you know he is fictitious. Ask her to set up Mr. Giraffe's dinner place in her room, for instance. This lets her know you are aware how vital he is but helps to draw a line between real and imaginary life.

Lay down the law, if needed. If your child blames Mr. Giraffe for mischief, you could say, "No matter who made the mess; you need to clean it up."

In the long term...

Help her develop real friendships. In addition to having Mr. Giraffe as a playmate, set up playdates so she can spend time with real peers, with all the negotiation, compromise, and fun that involves.

Listen in. By paying attention to your child's conversations with her imaginary playmate, you can get a sense of what's going on in her mind. Children can use imaginary friends to fulfill unmet needs or wishes they find hard to express to adults.

Remember it's a phase. Most imaginary friends fall out of favor after the age of 7 or 8 when pretend play also subsides. Despite the intensity of such relationships, many kids forget about their friend as they get older.

Moving away

To small children, home is their entire world, so the sight of it being dismantled in front of them can be overwhelming. By seeing the transition through your child's eyes, there's a lot you can do to help him settle sooner.

Moving is one of life's most stressful experiences. And while some children will view it as a huge adventure—depending on age, temperament, and circumstances—others will focus on the loss of leaving their old home and everything familiar.

Unless you explain it, children may also be confused by what's happening. For example, they may not realize that they can take all their belongings with them or that their pets can come, too. They may also be anxious to see the familiar objects they have grown up with—including their toys—disappear into huge boxes. If you're relocating, older children in particular will worry about starting a new school and finding new friends. Taking a little time to help your child understand what to expect can make the transition smoother for the whole family.

TELL YOUR CHILD THAT A HOME IS NOT ABOUT THE BUILDING BUT THE LOVE THAT HAPPENS INSIDE.

1
Prepare for change.
Take your child on a tour of your new home. Explain the process so he understands he is switching from living in one place to another, not going on vacation.

4
Let them make future plans.
To help your child feel more comfortable in his new home, give him as many safe choices as possible about how to make it cozy. Maybe he could choose the color of his new bedroom, arrange his stuffed animals, or decide where his bookcase goes.

6
Get childcare on moving day.
Moving is stressful for everyone, so ask a close friend, relative, or sitter to take your child out for the day. You'll be able to give him your full attention once everything is moved in.

GOOD PRACTICE
8 key principles

2
Explain why you are packing.
If you start putting children's things into huge boxes, your child may think they are disappearing for good or getting thrown away. Explain that they are just being stored safely for the move and he will see them again soon.

3
Enlist your child's help.
No matter your child's age, moving feels like a decision made by adults. Help your child feel more in control by asking her to help with packing, for example, by putting her favorite things in a special box. Let her draw or write on the boxes to keep her busy and to show what's inside.

5
Pack up their old room last and unpack the new one first.
Having a safe place with all his things at your new home will help your child feel more secure. Put his boxes into the moving van last so they are immediately at hand when you arrive.

7
Be upbeat.
Even if your family's new changes are the result of a job loss or parental separation, be upbeat. Children pick up on and take in parents' feelings. If you feel ready to make the best of it, so will they.

8
Stick to a routine.
Your child needs predictability to feel at home. Follow the usual bath and bedtime routine as soon as you're in your new place. This lets your child know that whatever else is changing, he can always rely on these things to happen.

Age by age

2–3
YEARS OLD

The right time
Leave explanations as late as you can but before the packing starts, so they're not living with the uncertainty for too long.

Avoiding overload
Hold off other stressful transitions, such as potty training, until your child has settled. Be understanding if he regresses, for example, by wanting a bottle.

4–5
YEARS OLD

Acting it out
Help your child understand the transition by role-playing with toy trucks, dollhouses, or shoeboxes to represent your old and new homes.

Story time subjects
There are many storybooks written for children about moving, which will help them understand the process.

6–7
YEARS OLD

Same but different
If your child has to change schools, take him on a tour beforehand. Emphasize that he will be learning similar things, so he won't be starting all over again.

New playmates
Get in touch with the school to arrange playdates with members of your child's class to help calm first-day nerves.

"I love being with you."

No one is more important in your child's life than you, and she never feels more secure than when she has your undivided attention. These moments of undistracted togetherness can be some of the most treasured times for both of you.

SCENARIO | You and your child are walking along together, holding hands.

SHE SAYS

"I love being with you."

When she was younger, your child expressed love physically, through hugs and snuggles. She recognizes what love means from the many times she has heard you say it to her. Now she is old enough to express this feeling back to you, spontaneously, with words as well as touch.

◆ SEE RELATED TOPICS ◆
You're always too busy: pp.128–129
You promised: pp.168–169

YOU MIGHT THINK

"This is such special time together. This is what parenting is all about."

WHAT SHE'S THINKING

"I love being with Mommy—especially when it's just the two of us."

A lot of parenting can be tedious or difficult, but the moments of tenderness you share with your child are pure delight. Your relationship can deepen as your child grows and becomes more of an active partner in your interactions, sharing her thoughts, feelings, and affection.

Although your child is now doing many things to show her independence, she still needs to refuel through times with you, talking and touching. Loving moments like these also release feel-good opioids in your child's brain, which will strengthen your bond.

HOW TO RESPOND

In the moment...

Share your love. Reflect back the same loving words so she knows you appreciate her spontaneous surge of affection. Just smile and answer warmly, "I love you, too!"

Savor the moment. Adults tend to be preoccupied with their schedules and to-do lists. Learn from your child how to find delight in small pleasures, such as walking hand in hand, balancing on a curb, spotting a caterpillar, or even pressing the button on an elevator.

Tell her you enjoy her company. This expresses your simple pleasure in being with her and shows that your love doesn't have to be earned.

In the long term...

Be responsive. Parents can't give children all their attention all the time—and kids don't want or need that—but you can make an effort to notice and respond with openness when your child reaches out to you.

Create opportunities. Parents are busier than ever, so you may need to deliberately plan undistracted times with her to make room for these precious moments of tender connection.

"Why is the sky blue?"

As children learn more about the world, they try to make sense of what they discover. How parents respond to their endless questions can help shape their wider understanding as well as help encourage their curiosity.

SCENARIO | **Your child is asking you a nonstop series of questions about the world while you're trying to get lunch ready.**

HE SAYS

"Why is the sky blue?"

YOU MIGHT THINK

"I'm glad he's curious, but these nonstop questions can get annoying."

At this age, children's brains are twice as active as adults', and your child now has a vocabulary of more than 2,000 words at his disposal. This expands his ability to enquire and means he may ask an average of 76 information-seeking questions per hour. He assumes that you have the answer to everything.

When your child seems like a bottomless pit of unrelated questions, you may get tired of being his on-demand encyclopedia. It's fine sometimes to say, "What do you think?" or "That's an interesting question. Let's talk about it after lunch."

WHEN CHILDREN ASK LOTS OF "WHY" QUESTIONS, YOUR PATIENCE AND ENCOURAGEMENT CAN HELP THEM FOSTER A LIFELONG LOVE OF LEARNING.

HOW TO RESPOND

In the moment...

①

Stop momentarily and listen. Often children will keep asking the same question if they don't get an answer that satisfies their curiosity. The answer doesn't have to be complicated. For instance, if your child asks, "Why are dogs furry?" you can answer, "To keep them warm."

②

Show how to find answers. When there's time, look for answers to your child's questions together. Use books or child-friendly online resources to explore topics he finds intriguing.

③

Figure out why he's asking. Studies show that most of the time your child genuinely wants answers. But if you think he is asking questions to avoid doing something he doesn't want to do, such as tidying up, reply: "That's a good question. I can answer it while you collect your puzzle pieces."

In the long term...

Stretch his mind. Occasionally responding to your child's question with a question can promote active reasoning. Asking "What do you think?" encourages him to draw upon what he knows to guess the answer.

Support growing expertise. Whether it's car models, dinosaur names, or flower types, knowing lots of facts about a chosen topic area gives kids an enjoyable sense of power. Support your child's interests through reading and family outings or activities that deepen his knowledge.

WHAT HE'S THINKING

"I want to understand everything, and I love chatting with Daddy!"

Children this age are eager to understand the world around them. They're also beginning to learn the back-and-forth of conversation. Your child enjoys asking and getting a response from you, and your answers also help him learn.

SEE RELATED TOPICS
When I was little...: pp.114–115
That's so funny!: pp.102–103

"But I didn't hear you."

One of the biggest frustrations for parents is when their children don't listen. It's exasperating to be ignored by your child, but shouting or nagging are upsetting for everyone. By giving effective directions, you can make it easier for your child to listen.

SCENARIO | Supper's ready, but despite telling your child several times that it's time to come in from the yard, she stays outside.

SHE SAYS

"But I didn't hear you."

YOU MIGHT THINK

"Why doesn't she just listen the first time?"

At this age, children tend to concentrate on one activity at a time. If your child is deeply absorbed in what she's doing, her brain may shut out anything that's not directly related. She may also have a hard time shifting from one activity to the next.

You may feel angry when your child doesn't listen and wonder if she's deliberately disrespecting you. But she's not thinking about you when she ignores your instructions. Instead of raising your voice or resorting to threats, give her the guidance she needs to switch gears.

" " TO GET YOUR CHILD'S COOPERATION, MAKE IT EASIER FOR HER TO LISTEN.

SEE RELATED TOPICS
I'm just going to do it: pp.100–101
I don't want to clean up: pp.148–149

WHAT SHE'S THINKING

"I'm having so much fun! I just want to keep playing."

Sometimes parents accidentally teach their kids not to listen. If you routinely ask your child 15 times to do something, she learns that she can ignore you the first 14 times, because you don't really expect her to respond until the 15th request.

HOW TO RESPOND

In the moment...

(1)

Be clear. Directions shouted from afar are easy to ignore. Walk over, gently touch her shoulder, make eye contact, and give one polite instruction as a statement, not a question. Tell her what she should do rather than what she shouldn't. "Dinner is ready. Please come in."

(2)

Help her shift. If she's enjoying what she's doing, ease the transition by telling her, "Do your last thing," and then stay nearby to guide her to the next activity.

(3)

Say thanks. Smile and thank her when she does good listening. Give a hug or a high five if it took some effort.

In the long term...

Have her say it. If your child tends to get distracted, have her repeat your instruction after you say it, to make sure she's heard and understood it. Ask, "What's your job right now?"

Make it fun. Getting kids to listen doesn't have to be serious. A playful approach, such as asking in a silly voice, using an oven mitt puppet, or turning the job into a game makes cooperation appealing.

"When I was little..."

While the memory centers in your child's brain are developing, he won't necessarily remember all the events he recalls now when he's older. But even though he may forget some things, such sharing of memories will boost his confidence and shape his view of the world.

SCENARIO | **Your child has surprised you by remembering an event during a vacation last summer, when he was 3.**

HE SAYS

"When I was little..."

YOU MIGHT THINK

"I thought he would have forgotten that by now."

At this age, your child is beginning to grasp the ideas of past, present, and future. He can remember and talk about events from the past, especially ones that stand out as happy, sad, or scary. He's still a bit unclear about how long ago something happened, so "when I was little" is a convenient label for anything that happened a while ago.

As your child's verbal skills increase, he becomes better at recording, retaining, and retrieving memories. He is developing a more elaborate autobiographical memory that will help form his sense of self and his role within the family.

"" ""

HELPING YOUR CHILD REMEMBER THE FUN TIMES, AS WELL AS THE CHALLENGES, WILL HELP HIM LEARN FROM THE PAST AND MAKE SENSE OF THE FUTURE.

WHAT HE'S THINKING

"It's fun to think about before and now and see how I've changed."

Your child's abilities are expanding rapidly at this age, so he enjoys comparing his current self to his past self and seeing his progress. He also enjoys reliving happy events. When you talk about past events together, you help him elaborate and reinforce his memories.

HOW TO RESPOND

In the moment...

①

Listen to the memories. Pay attention and ask for more details. What was he thinking or feeling at the time? This helps him feel important, reinforces his memories, and validates the way he experiences the world.

②

Fill in the gaps. Children often need help retrieving memories at this age. Show him photos and retell the event as if it was a story that happened to him. This will also help him learn sequencing, a skill that helps with logical thinking and understanding cause and effect.

In the long term...

Make them interesting. Children tend to remember the things they find most interesting. When you refer back to an event, choose questions that prompt memorable details, such as "Do you remember we went to the place with the pirate caves?" or "Whose ice cream was stolen by the seagull?"

Put memories in context. The human brain tends to put more emphasis on negative memories. If your child tends to dwell more on these—for instance, talking about falling off his bike on that vacation—acknowledge the memory. But also help him feel more positive with reminders of the fun times, too, so he builds a balanced picture of the world.

Show him how far he's come. Talk about your child's memories so he takes pride in how far he's come in life. By pointing out that on vacation he was still learning to ride a bike but now rides it smoothly, you can show appreciation for his ability to master new skills.

> **SEE RELATED TOPICS**
>
> **Are you sad, Mommy?:** pp.96–97
> **Why is the sky blue?:** pp.110–111

"I give up."

Resilience is the ability to cope with challenges and bounce back from disappointment. To develop this skill, your child will need to have many experiences of learning to overcome small setbacks, so she's willing and able to handle bigger challenges.

SCENARIO | **Your child is trying to glue two boxes together to make a model. When it doesn't work, she storms off.**

SHE SAYS

"I give up."

YOU MIGHT THINK

"She needs to learn to keep trying. I don't want her to be a quitter!"

Your child has an idea of how she wants the model to look, but her hands can't make what her mind sees. As her frustration builds to the point of helplessness, she may even smash the boxes because they're not doing what she wants.

You know how important persistence is in life, and you also see how upset your child is. But if you leap in to rescue her by fixing the model for her, you steal her opportunity to learn important coping skills. Your job is to guide her toward persevering rather than take over.

◆ SEE RELATED TOPICS ▶
Was that good?: pp.164–165
I want it to be perfect: pp.172–173

WHAT SHE'S THINKING

"I can't do it! I'll never be able to do it. It's too hard for me."

For young children, a frustrated "It's not working!" can easily slip into a helpless "I can't do anything right!" You can help your child move past this crisis moment and enable her to keep trying or revise her goals in a more realistic direction.

HOW TO RESPOND

In the moment...

Calm first. Encourage her to step away from the project. A short break will help her settle down and avoid doing something destructive. Describe her feelings to make them more understandable and therefore more manageable. "You're frustrated that the boxes won't stay together." Then distract her with a book, toy, or snack to help her regroup.

Urge flexible thinking. After she's calm, ask questions to help her consider other strategies. "The glue isn't working. What else could you use to attach the boxes?"

In the long term...

Read inspiring stories. Classics such as *The Little Engine That Could* can help her understand the value of persisting in the face of challenges.

Describe when she manages to persist. For example, you could say, "This was a hard puzzle. Sometimes you had to try several pieces before finding the right one. But you kept going, and now you've finished the whole thing!"

Know when to switch gears. Although persistence is valuable, sometimes quitting is the wisest choice. For example, if an activity turns out not to be a good match for her, it's okay to shift to something that's a better fit.

"I'm scared of the dark."

As your child's imagination takes flight and he becomes more aware of the wider world around him, your 4- to 5-year-old is starting to have new fears, which may surprise you. One of the most common is fear of the dark.

SCENARIO | Your child won't go to sleep because he's scared when his bedroom light is turned off.

HE SAYS

"I'm scared of the dark."

YOU MIGHT THINK

"He has slept in this room for a while. Why is he suddenly scared?"

Fear of the dark affects about half of children at this age. Although it's not helpful for modern parents, such fear once served a useful evolutionary role. At an age when children become more curious and more physically able to explore the world, it stops them from wandering off at night and getting lost or, worse, eaten by a predator.

Usually a fearful phase fades away within a few months. So avoid dismissing your child's fears as a cry for attention. If his worries are dismissed or met with anger and frustration, he may become more scared.

CHILDREN CAN LEARN TO
MANAGE THEIR FEARS OF
THE UNKNOWN AND SOOTHE
THEMSELVES WHEN GROWN-
UPS SHOW THEM HOW.

WHAT HE'S THINKING

"What if there's something scary hiding in the dark?"

Your child's fear is real because the darkness means he can't see familiar objects or environments that reassure him he's safe. What's more: his anxiety may make him alert to every creak in the house or noises from outside. With fewer distractions at night, his imagination can run wild.

HOW TO RESPOND

In the moment...

Ask questions. Get him to talk about his feelings and listen so you can understand exactly what he is afraid of. Summarize and repeat back to him what he's saying so he knows you have heard and understood. By helping to name his worries, he will feel more in charge.

Make his room a haven. Your child's room needs to feel like a safe place, so never send him there as a punishment. A regular bedtime routine creates certainty of what comes next and when the room light goes off. Keep his door open so that there aren't any barriers between him and you, which will offer him extra comfort.

Adjust the lighting. Buy your child a night-light, possibly in the form of a friendly animal, which will make him feel safe and will cast a warm glow within his room so he can see his familiar things around him and feel reassured.

In the long term...

Check his viewing history. Has your child seen older siblings or friends play older-age video games, or has he seen scary movies or heard ghost stories that are feeding his fears? Sometimes overhearing or catching a glimpse of TV news can also be enough to trigger worries in children this age.

Help him change the story. At other times of the day, not before bedtime, read him a story in which he is the main character who overcomes a fear, such as a monster or the darkness. Find a story that can help him process fears during daylight hours.

SEE RELATED TOPICS

Sleep difficulties: pp.74–75
I had a bad dream: pp.140–141

"I'm telling."

Rules help children know the right thing to do. At this age, your child is a black-and-white thinker, so a broken rule seems completely unacceptable—especially if she didn't do it. She tattles to show you she's good and knows your rules and to try to get you on her side.

SCENARIO | **Your child keeps coming to you to complain that her playmate is not putting the lid back on the glue during a craft session.**

SHE SAYS

"I'm telling."

Tattling is an in-between step for kids who have enough self-control to refrain from hitting a peer but can't yet problem solve on their own. It's very common among preschoolers. Your child won't grasp the social costs of tattling until after age 6.

" "

IT WILL TAKE YEARS FOR YOUR CHILD TO FIGURE OUT WHEN TO REPORT PEERS' MISBEHAVIOR TO AN ADULT AND WHEN TO LET IT SLIDE.

YOU MIGHT THINK

"Why is she tattling on her friend about such a minor thing?"

You want your child to tell you if there's a real problem, but tattling about minor "crimes" is annoying to adults and peers. As a teen, she'll avoid reporting peers' misbehavior. But at this age, it's hard for her to resist telling you when something is wrong. If her tattling works to pull you to intervene, she'll do it more.

HOW TO RESPOND

In the moment...

(1)

Teach guidelines. Make a poster illustrating three questions: "Is someone hurt? Is something broken? Have you tried two times to handle it?" Use it to help her think through whether she should come to you. If the answer is no to all of these, she's tattling to get someone in trouble, not telling to be helpful, so you won't step in.

(2)

Give her options. Your child doesn't know what to do when someone breaks a rule, other than tattle. Explain how she can handle the situation herself. For example, "Use your words to tell him you want a turn," "You can put the lid back on," or "Play with something else."

(3)

Make tattling less satisfying. Don't leap to fix things. For minor complaints, respond with, "Hmm," then turn away. For heated complaints, ask, "Can you play together peacefully, or do you need to play separately?"

In the long term...

Refocus. At this age, your child's conscience is centered on rules. It's upsetting to her to see someone break a rule that she has to follow. Tell her, "You're in charge of what you do; not what others do." Insist that correcting other kids is a job only for grown-ups. If you didn't see the bad behavior happen, you won't step in.

Catch her coping. Children this age don't recognize that tattling irritates other children. Older kids identify more with peers than adults, so they tattle less. In the meantime, notice and applaud when your child copes on her own. "You solved the problem all by yourself!"

WHAT SHE'S THINKING

"She's breaking the rule! I have to tell a grown-up."

Pointing out that someone else is breaking the rules makes your child feel virtuous. By announcing, "She's bad, and I'm good!" she hopes to get your attention and approval. She may also want to get you on her side or get the other child in trouble. She's genuinely bothered that the rules aren't being followed and doesn't know how else to handle it.

◀ SEE RELATED TOPICS ▶
They called me a crybaby: pp.138–139
You can't come to my party: pp.152–153

Car trips

Trips can be boring and difficult for children: it's a big ask to be physically restrained when they're full of energy. But by understanding where your child is developmentally, you can make travel more pleasant for the whole family.

Younger children do not yet understand the abstract concept of time—or how long an hour lasts—which can lead to repeated and exasperating "Are we there yet?" questions. They also do not yet understand time and distance, so they get frustrated when they don't know how long they will have to sit in a restricted seat.

But, rather than viewing them as torments to be endured, long car trips can offer great opportunities for parents and children to relax and have fun together.

That said, while they are still learning impulse control and patience, not every trip will be problem-free. Throw siblings into the mix, and restlessness and fights can escalate in no time. So being well prepared can help reduce the stress of traveling and make trips more enjoyable.

1
Sort snacks and entertainment ahead of time.
Before a big trip, ask your child what he would like to bring with him to help pass the time—his "bag of fun." This could include audiobooks, music, activity books, or travel-friendly toys or games.

4
Insist on seat belts.
Some children hate being restrained by seat belts for long periods, but, here, compromise is not an option. Explain that wearing a seat belt helps keep them safe.

6
Don't just rely on screens.
If you believe screens will be helpful for a trip, it's still wise to set limits. Otherwise, your child will expect to be entertained with devices at all times, even on short trips. Decide beforehand and tell him that you will let him watch a movie or a TV episode at a certain point in the trip.

GOOD PRACTICE
8 key principles

2
Form a united front.
Plan with your partner how you want to handle common problems—sibling fights and requests for screens. Make an effort to be kind to each other because seeing parental fights at such close range can be alarming for young children.

3
Interact with everyone.
View car trips as a time to be together and talk. To make the trip go faster, play interactive games, such as I Spy or license plate spotting, or look out for landmarks, colors, and different-shaped clouds.

5
Deal with siblings separately.
If sibling fighting gets serious, pull over and deal with it. Listen to each child's side and ask how you can make the rest of the trip better. If you have adult help, take each child for a short walk to let off steam. Once they are back in the car, place a barrier between them or keep them out of touching distance.

7
Take frequent breaks.
It's tempting to push through to get to your destination quickly, but letting everyone get out and stretch his or her legs every hour or two will help keep the peace. Look for places to stop at parks, service stations, or playgrounds on the way.

8
Anticipate car sickness.
Children may get car sick if they can't see out or, if they are older, they are fixing their focus on a book or a device. Motion sickness arises when the inner ear senses movement but the eyes and body don't, leading to feelings of nausea. Encourage your child to look out the front window and distract him with talking games and stories.

TAILORED ADVICE
Age by age

2–3
YEARS OLD

PJs at the ready
If you've got a long car trip ahead, think about setting off in the evening or before dawn so your child sleeps for a lot of it.

Bring surprises
Have a new sticker book or a toy your child hasn't played with in a while ready to pull out when he gets cranky.

4–5
YEARS OLD

Musical moments
Children this age love to show what they know. Play their favorite songs and then stop the music so they can finish it off.

Are we there yet?
Use simple markers of time your child can understand. For example, "We'll be there after we've eaten lunch" or "...when the fields turn into a town."

6–7
YEARS OLD

Map reading
Your child now has the spatial understanding to follow a map. To make the trip go more easily, give him a spare map and challenge him to follow the route with his finger. This will give him a sense of control over where he is going and allow him to work out how far you've come.

"You love her more."

Your children are different people with different needs and personalities, so of course you're not going to treat them exactly the same. They'll find it easier to tolerate unavoidable inequality if they understand your reasons and believe you're generally fair.

SCENARIO | When your child doesn't get her own way about which movie to watch, she says you love her sibling more.

How you respond to sibling jealousy and rivalry can intensify or minimize this tension. Favoritism hurts children and causes resentment. But trying to make everything perfectly equal communicates that even small differences are unbearable. Siblings want to be different enough to be special but similar enough to have a sense of belonging. Sensitive parenting requires meeting each child's needs while being as fair as possible about conflicts. Sibling rivalry shows up in two main ways:

● **Fighting for your attention** happens when children feel that a sibling is intruding on her loving relationship with you. This kind of jealousy is affected by your relationship with each child as well as the children's relationship with each other.

● **Fighting over property** happens when kids defend their turf or seek power, revenge, or novelty by taking their sibling's things.

◀ SEE RELATED TOPICS ▶
I hate her: pp.130–131
I never wanted a little brother: pp.134–135

" "

SIBLINGS DON'T WANT TO BE LOVED EQUALLY; THEY EACH WANT TO BE LOVED SPECIALLY.

THE ROUTE TO FOLLOW

Assessing sibling rivalry

FIGHTING FOR YOUR ATTENTION

SIGNS

Jumping on you or timing disruptive behavior for when you are with the other child.

Accusing you of favoritism and saying you love the other child more.

Asking who you love best.

TRIGGERS

Bedtimes when the older child is allowed to stay up later.

Arguments over who gets to sit next to you at mealtimes.

When you're helping or playing with the other sibling.

Hearing praise of her sibling.

When only one child goes with you on an errand.

RESPONSE

1. **Acknowledge her jealousy.** Say, "That feels unfair to you" or "You wish you could do it, too." Don't dismiss jealousy or say there's no cause for it.

2. **Express your love.** Tell her she's the only one you love in her special way. List unique and unearned qualities you adore, such as her smile or curiosity.

3. **Explain why** when a sibling needs extra attention, such as when she's ill, so your child knows it's temporary and not a rejection of her.

4. **Set aside the same amount of special time** with Daddy and Mommy for each child every day.

5. **Don't compare siblings,** even in a positive way. It sends the message that they are in competition.

FIGHTING OVER PROPERTY

SIGNS

Tugs of war and grabbing their sibling's toys or possessions.

Physical fights and ruining games.

Using others' possessions without permission.

TRIGGERS

Boredom.

Desire to exercise power.

Jealousy of sibling and desire for revenge.

Wish to control how to play a game.

Frustration leading to destructive urges.

RESPONSE

1. **Don't take sides,** or one child will think she has lost and the other has won, triggering more hostility between them. Assume that they share the blame.

2. **Ask if they have any ideas** for how to resolve the conflict. If they think of some, give plenty of praise.

3. **Encourage games** that take teamwork. Children will bond more if they are striving for a common goal, for example, building a fort.

4. **Give them personal space,** such as a "treasures" shelf, to keep toys they don't want to share.

5. **Call family meetings.** Create a regular forum to make sure all children can express their thoughts, feelings, and wishes, and be heard.

"I lost teddy."

Your child is working on becoming more independent from you, his parent. But he may still want the extra security of an object, such as a stuffed animal or a blanket, to comfort him when you're not with him.

SCENARIO | **You're trying to leave the house, but your child refuses to come because he can't find his favorite toy.**

HE SAYS

"I lost teddy."

YOU MIGHT THINK

"We need to go now. We don't have time to look for teddy."

Between the ages of 8 months and 1 year, your child began to understand that you couldn't always be with him. To bridge this gap, he adopted a favorite toy or object. This is a source of comfort and security, so it can be hard to be without it.

Teddy is an important part of your child's development and shows that he is working out ways to comfort himself. Respect your child's attachment to his toy, but don't let it get in the way of daily life.

CHILDREN HANG ON TO SPECIAL TOYS TO HELP THEM FEEL COMFORTED.

WHAT HE'S THINKING

"I'm scared that teddy's gone forever! I need him."

Your child's attachment to teddy is not a sign of insecurity or weakness. Instead, teddy is a companion who is helping your child make the transition from dependence to independence by helping him feel safe when he goes to bed or faces new situations.

SEE RELATED TOPICS
I do it!: pp.38–39
I'm scared of the dark: pp.118–119

HOW TO RESPOND

In the moment...

Show that you understand. When teddy goes missing, calmly tell your child that you know he loves teddy and you'll help him look for teddy when you get back. Reassure him that teddy will be safe, waiting for him to return.

Set boundaries. Your child is caught up in his worries of the moment, but you see the bigger picture. You may have to insist, gently but firmly, that it's time to go. He may let you help him write a note to teddy saying he'll be back soon.

Distract him. If your child is upset that he has to leave home without teddy, distract him with plenty of talk, songs, and games. You can also ask him which other toy he'd like to bring, just while he's waiting to find teddy.

In the long term...

Double up. If your child takes teddy everywhere, there's always the risk that teddy will get lost or wrecked. Buy an identical backup in case teddy is misplaced, and then you also have a substitute when you have to wash the original. Swap them from time to time so both smell and feel the same.

Scale it down. Most children will give up attachment objects by themselves by the age of about 6 as they start to see them as babyish. If you feel your child needs help to go it alone, suggest keeping teddy at home just for bedtimes. Or if his security object is a blanket, see if he'll let you cut it into smaller squares to keep in his pocket.

"You're always too busy."

Spending time with your child is crucial, but the most important thing is to be responsive. When your child seeks your attention, try to respond with warmth and interest. Turning toward our kids more often than away builds their sense of security and closeness.

SCENARIO | **When your child asks you to come and play, you tell her you have to finish your online grocery shopping.**

SHE SAYS

"You're always too busy."

YOU MIGHT THINK

"I wish I could play with her, but there's so much to do."

At this age, what your child experiences right now feels like what is "always" true. She's eager to play with you and frustrated that you can't drop everything to do what she wants. It's hard for her to wait, but if you keep your promise when you're done, she'll learn.

As parents, we're pulled in many directions: childcare, chores, work, and the needs of the family can get in the way of playing. But we have to guard against letting our endless to-do list push out responding to and delighting in our children.

ASK FOR HELP FROM YOUR CO-PARENT AND FAMILY. IT TAKES A VILLAGE TO RAISE A CHILD, NOT ONE EXHAUSTED ADULT.

HOW TO RESPOND

In the moment...

Let her help. Show your child what you're doing and explain why. Involve her, if you can, or let her keep you company by doing something near you until you're done.

Set a timer so she knows how long she has to wait until you're free. Try to keep it under 15 minutes. It may help to have a box of "while-you're-waiting" toys or crafts set aside for these moments. Honor your promise when the timer goes off.

In the long term...

Build in daily one-on-one time. No parent can spend every moment of every day playing, but setting aside even 15 minutes a day to give her your undivided attention and to do what she enjoys can be something you both look forward to.

Watch out for digital distractors. Phones and laptops can be distracting or even hypnotizing. Let your child see you put them away so you can be fully present when you're doing things with her.

Take care of yourself so you can take care of her. You can't be the kind of parent you want to be if you're running on empty. If you're often feeling short-tempered, overwhelmed, or resentful at how much you have to do, try to figure out who can help or how you can lighten your load. Take steps to refuel by getting needed sleep or exercise or setting aside time for yourself with a book, bath, hobbies, or friends.

WHAT SHE'S THINKING

"I want Mommy to play with me right now!"

Your child doesn't understand your obligations, so of course she's upset that you can't play whenever she wants. Even if you're busy, you can still respond warmly to her bids for your attention. If you have to say, "Not right now," give her a smile and a hug, and tell her, "That sounds fun! Let's do it soon," to ease her disappointment.

SEE RELATED TOPICS

Look what I did!: pp.92–93
I love being with you: pp.108–109

"I hate her."

Studies find that siblings aged 3 to 7 average 3½ conflicts per hour. So if you feel like your kids are at each other all the time, it's because sometimes they really are. Their battles can get heated, but it's the fun they have together that predicts whether siblings will be close.

SCENARIO | **Your younger child says he hates his 7-year-old sister after she banishes him from her room for being "annoying."**

HE SAYS

"I hate her."

Hearing children use the word "hate" about a sibling is upsetting for parents, but it's normal for kids to feel an intense mix of conflicting emotions about their siblings. They can be playful or tender with each other, but they can also be hostile. Kids' most aggressive conflicts tend to be with siblings, because they're stuck with each other and often believe that meanness to a sibling doesn't count.

" "
SIBLING RELATIONSHIPS CAN TEACH CHILDREN LIFELONG SKILLS, SUCH AS SHARING.

SEE RELATED TOPICS

I'm so mad!: pp.98–99
She's not listening: pp.146–147

YOU MIGHT THINK

"I hoped my children would grow up to be friends. How has it come to this?"

WHAT HE'S THINKING

"She's mean! She shouldn't tell me to go away."

We want our kids to be good buddies, so it's disappointing and aggravating to see them be mean to each other. Your own experiences growing up may color how you react to sibling squabbles, perhaps making you more sensitive to one child's view than another's.

The eyes point outward, so both kids will likely be thinking about the other's misdeeds rather than their own contribution to the conflict. But keep in mind that their feelings can change quickly. If his sister asked him to play now, he'd likely leap to accept.

HOW TO RESPOND

In the moment...

Acknowledge his feelings. Don't argue about whether he truly hates his sister. "Hate" is just a catch-all word for his intense emotions. Help him label his feelings and distinguish among disappointed, frustrated, angry, or sad. It's easier to cope when he knows you understand.

Guide them toward resolution. Instead of choosing sides or proclaiming a solution, ask, "What would be fair to both of you?" If they're being cruel or physically hurtful, say, "It's not safe for you to be together right now. You can talk things out later, when you're feeling calmer."

Avoid labeling their relationship negatively. Don't let your children hear you say they "don't get along," or they will define their relationship the same way.

In the long term...

Create chances for them to have fun together. Get your children to collaborate on a project, such as making a tent out of sheets, or try kids-against-the-grown-up(s) games to make them allies and bring them closer.

Encourage empathy. Help both children understand the other's perspective. Brainstorm kind ways to handle difficult situations or ask for what they want.

"I feel sad."

Parents often imagine that children's lives are so carefree that they should be happy all the time, apart from the odd meltdown when they don't get their way. But your child will experience a range of emotions throughout her day.

SCENARIO | As you walk home from school, you notice your child is quiet and seems downcast.

SHE SAYS

"I feel sad."

YOU MIGHT THINK

"Oh, no! What happened? I want her to be happy!"

Children tend to experience emotions more intensely than adults, perhaps because they haven't lived long enough to have perspective. This means sadness, anger, or fear may feel overwhelming. By talking openly, your child is showing her trust in you to comfort and help.

You may feel worried to hear your child say she's feeling sad, because of course you don't want her to suffer. Although you want to give her a happy childhood, it's also important to help her learn to cope with the negative emotions that are an unavoidable part of life.

HELP YOUR CHILD UNDERSTAND THAT EMOTIONS COME AND GO. THERE ARE WAYS TO MANAGE FEELINGS.

WHAT SHE'S THINKING

"Something made me feel bad today, and now my body feels heavy and I feel sad."

Being able to recognize and label emotions is an important skill and can guide coping efforts. At this age, your child realizes that events can affect how she feels. She has also worked out that sadness feels like a mix of disappointment, loss, low energy, and perhaps tearfulness.

HOW TO RESPOND

In the moment...

Accept her feelings. Don't try to talk her out of being sad. Ask what happened so she can piece together the sequence of events. This retelling will help her make sense of her jumbled feelings. Describe the feelings you hear: "You felt sad and mad when she did that."

Give her space. If she doesn't want to tell you what happened, don't push. Just say, "When you're ready to tell me, I'd like to hear." Give her a hug, and ask again later. She may be more open to telling you at bedtime.

Tell her that feelings pass. While she may feel sad now, it doesn't mean she'll feel sad all the time. After acknowledging her feelings, you can coach her in how to cope. Ask what she thinks might help. Distraction, speaking up, making a plan, or just letting time pass are all possibilities you can help her consider.

In the long term...

Connect feelings to the body. Children understand emotions through their bodies. When she's emotional, ask, "What do you feel in your body?" Restless? Heavy? Tense? Doing something physical can also shift her emotional state. Running around outside can energize her; taking slow, deep breaths can calm her.

Talk about others' feelings. When parents talk more about feelings, as they come up in daily life or in books or movies, children become better able to understand their own and others' emotional experiences. When you calmly discuss your own emotions, you show your child that everyone has feelings and they're safe to talk about.

SEE RELATED TOPICS
I'm so mad!: pp.98–99
I want it to be perfect: pp.172–173

"I never wanted a little brother."

A new baby in the family is a big change for everyone. Your child not only has to adjust to the presence of a new little person who doesn't do much beyond sleep, eat, and poop, but he also has to deal with the fact that you're more exhausted and distracted.

SCENARIO | **You are delighted to have just welcomed your second child into the family.**

HE SAYS

"I never wanted a little brother."

You probably decided to have another child partly because you hoped your kids would be buddies. That may happen, but right now, your older child sees mostly just the disruption caused by the arrival of the new baby.

SEE RELATED TOPICS
I love being with you: pp.108–109
You love her more: pp.124–125

YOU MIGHT THINK

"I was so hoping he would love the baby."

WHAT HE'S THINKING

"I want things to be back to the way they were."

It's very common for older siblings to tell parents they want to send the baby back. This doesn't mean your child is permanently rejecting the baby; he's just struggling to adjust to the changes. You may feel guilty about his distress, but with your loving support, he'll adjust.

Children vary in how they respond to a new baby, but change is difficult for everyone. Your child probably feels a mix of emotions: excited and jealous, curious and annoyed, eager to please and frustrated. He needs you to accept the full range of his feelings.

HOW TO RESPOND

In the moment...

Read together. Books about a new baby can help your child understand and express the confusing bundle of emotions he's probably having. Tell him, "Things have changed a lot, but you'll always be my special Matthew."

Roll with regression. New older siblings often revert to babyish behavior. He may go backward on potty training or insist that you feed or dress him. Go along with his wishes. This will pass. Don't tell him, "You're the big brother now." Kids have mixed feelings about being big.

In the long term...

Stay connected. Carry your newborn in a sling so your hands are free to play with him. Let him be involved in caring for the baby. Give him your full attention when the baby is sleeping.

Get others involved. Remind guests to pay attention to him as well as the baby. They should greet him first and remark on how lucky the baby is to have him as a brother.

Point out his biggest fan. Put his finger in the baby's hand. When the baby grabs it, say, "Oh, he likes you!" Talk about how the baby loves to watch him play. Tell him he's good at comforting the baby with a song or gentle pats.

Dealing with a sick child

Children get lots of minor illnesses in their early years as they build up their immunity. Whatever the ailment, your sympathy and practical help will ease your child's recovery.

When your child gets sick, you may experience a range of reactions, including concern, frustration, or stress. It can often be hard to assess how sick she is when she says, "I don't feel well" or "My tummy hurts," because she doesn't yet have all the words to describe how she feels.

Because parents want to be as kind as possible, they may also wonder about whether the usual routines and expectations of behavior should still apply during short periods of illness.

If you're in any doubt about how sick your child is, seek professional advice.

HELP YOUR CHILD STAY CALM ABOUT AN ILLNESS BY BEING CALM AND REASSURING YOURSELF.

1
Take care of yourself.
If you get sick, too, it'll be harder for you to care for your child. Wash your hands and get enough sleep so your immune system stays strong.

4
Focus on prevention.
Teach your child to sneeze and cough into her elbow and wash her hands before meals and after using the bathroom to minimize illness.

7
Stick to boundaries.
As much as possible, keep family rules in place—for instance, no hitting siblings and a limit on screen time. If rules do slip, return to your usual expectations as soon as you can.

9
Remember siblings.
If a child is sick for a while, make sure any other siblings are not feeling left out. Arrange special times to focus on them.

10 key principles

2
Talk about getting better.
Discuss with your child how strong her body is and how good it is at healing itself. If you need to talk to others about her illness, do so out of her earshot.

3
Check guidelines.
Not every illness means keeping your child out of school. Ask yourself: "Is my child too sick to join in activities?" "Does she have something contagious?" "Would I take a day off if I had it?" If the answer is yes to any of these, keep her home.

5
Avoid big reactions.
Listen when your child says she has an ache or pain. But try not to get overanxious or emotional when she complains, as this may reinforce inappropriate attention-seeking.

6
Give lots of cuddles.
When your child is sick, she may regress to more infantile behavior and want to be more attached to you. Respond accordingly.

8
Juggle work demands.
A sick child can be extra stressful for working parents. Know your company's rules so you can plan how you'll handle your child's illnesses. If possible, enlist your partner's help, too.

10
Notice body language.
Children sometimes express emotions via their bodies. Watch for patterns in headaches or tummyaches that might signal stress. If your child recovers miraculously when you say she can stay home, she may be avoiding difficult classwork or friendship issues. She may also feel jealous of a sibling who stays home or anxious about leaving you. Offer your help, support, and extra loving, but rely mostly on objective signs, such as fever, to decide whether she needs to go.

TAILORED ADVICE
Age by age

2–3
YEARS OLD

Be patient
A sick child is often a cranky child. Try to stay calm and kind, even if your child is irritable, and do what you can to make her comfortable.

Out of bed
Young children can run fevers and simultaneously want to run around. If you can't keep them in bed, don't worry.

4–5
YEARS OLD

Easy does it
After an illness, some children may feel nervous about returning to school. Reassure them that it will feel the same as before.

Root cause
Studies have found that at this age, children have limited understanding of the causes of illness. Read a book together about how the body fights off germs.

6–7
YEARS OLD

Explain procedures
Research finds that when 6-year-olds are sick, they may believe medical treatment is a kind of punishment unless someone explains how it helps them get better.

It's catching
By 7, children become aware that some illnesses can be "caught" from others. Let them know what kind of illness they have and what causes it.

"They called me a crybaby."

Children start to cry less at about the age of 2, when they can start to use words to express how they feel and explain what they want or need. However, some children are temperamentally more sensitive and more prone to tears.

SCENARIO | Your child tells you his classmates don't want to play with him because they say he's a crybaby.

HE SAYS

"They called me a crybaby."

YOU MIGHT THINK

"Why does he cry so easily and often?"

Your child may not yet realize that while crying gets sympathy from adults, his peers find it annoying. When he bursts into tears, it interrupts the flow of their game, and adults tend to intervene. Then his peers get angry with him for "spoiling" the fun.

Everyone cries sometimes, but if your child often cries around other kids, it could mean that he hasn't learned more effective ways to cope. Frequent crying can trigger teasing and get in the way of learning and having fun. You can't force your child to stop crying, but you can help him learn to manage his emotions.

YOUR ROLE ISN'T TO MAKE YOUR CHILD DEVELOP A THICK SKIN BUT TO HELP HIM LEARN TO MANAGE HOW HE RESPONDS.

HOW TO RESPOND

In the moment...

Help him manage the tears. Show your child how breathing slowly can calm him down. Help him practice—breathing in through his nose and out through his mouth. Such breathing slows the release of adrenaline and will help him stay calmer and more logical.

Be gender neutral. Don't tell him not to cry because he's a "big boy." Boys need to be able to express their feelings just as much as girls.

Help him gain perspective. While encouraging him to talk about how he feels, train him to keep minor upsets in perspective. Ask, "Is this problem big or little? Is it forever or just today?"

Acknowledge his feelings. When you put his feelings into words, your caring response makes them seem less overwhelming. Also, talk about how it can be more comforting to shed tears among close family and friends than among children who may not understand.

In the long term...

Teach him other coping strategies. Help him make a plan for situations that might make him cry, such as losing a game, not being allowed to join in, or being teased. He could speak up, walk away, play with someone else, delay his response by counting to 10, or distract himself by noticing all the blue items nearby.

WHAT HE'S THINKING

"When I get upset, my tears come out. I can't help it."

Your child may simply find it harder to control his feelings. Research has found that 15–20 percent of children come into the world with a more sensitive temperament. They often start by being more easily startled as babies and may grow into children who are more easily distressed. But learning to cope can change his inborn tendencies.

SEE RELATED TOPICS
I'm scared of the dark: pp.118–119
I'm telling: pp.120–121

"I had a bad dream."

Although parents wish their children sweet dreams, most children will have the occasional nightmare. At the age of 4 and 5, about three-fourths of children have frightening dreams from time to time, with some having as many as one or two a week.

SCENARIO | Your child has woken up in the night distressed, saying she was lost and being chased by a monster.

SHE SAYS

"I had a bad dream."

Children experience more rapid eye movement (REM) sleep—a type of deep sleep in which dreaming occurs—than adults. Dreams are a sign of increasing sophistication in the brain, building up a bigger memory bank and processing more fears as she learns more about the world.

YOU MIGHT THINK

"What's causing this bad dream? Is something bothering her?"

Seeing your child distressed is upsetting, heightened by the fact that you're startled awake in the middle of the night. Bad dreams can result from watching something scary or from a troublesome worry and are more common at times of upheaval—such as starting a new school or family discord.

SEE RELATED TOPICS
I'm scared of the dark: pp.118–119
I wet the bed: pp.158–159

" "

TELL YOUR CHILD IT'S POSSIBLE TO CHANGE THE STORY OF A BAD DREAM AND GIVE IT A HAPPY ENDING.

WHAT SHE'S THINKING

"Did the things in my bad dream really happen?"

Since your child's still developing the ability to tell the difference between real and imaginary, nightmares feel as if they really happened. She doesn't know that such bad dreams are created in her own imagination as her brain tries to process what's gone on in her day.

HOW TO RESPOND

In the moment...

Stay calm and reassure. Children can find it hard to calm down after a bad dream. Offer empathy and distraction. Cuddle her, and in a soothing way, say: "How scary that must have felt. It's all over now. It wasn't real." Keep interaction brief, though, so she can quickly fall back to sleep.

Encourage her to stay where she is. Rather than let her come into bed with you, try to calm your child so she goes back to sleep in her own room and learns to soothe herself in her own surroundings.

In the long term...

Talk about her feelings in the light of day. If she talks more about her emotions when she is with you, it may allow her to process her experiences during the daylight hours when it feels less disturbing, and a reason may emerge. She may like to draw about it, too.

Help her get enough sleep. A consistent bedtime routine, a cuddle, and a favorite book before bed will help your child feel more secure and relaxed for a good night's sleep.

Check what she's watching. Your child's nightmares may stem from seeing films, video games, or news items that are too old for her. Be careful to screen out any images she is not ready for.

"I didn't do it."

From time to time, nearly all children will tell untruths, omit details, or exaggerate. Research finds that, on average, 2-year-olds lie every five hours, 4-year-olds lie every two hours, and 6-year-olds lie every hour and a half. Your responses can guide your child toward honesty.

SCENARIO | You see your child push his friend over, but he denies it.

Lying is usually undesirable, but it's also a sign of cognitive development. To lie, your child has to be able to imagine and convey something untrue, anticipate the listener's reaction to hearing it, and stick to his story. Older kids lie more often and more believably than younger ones.

Preschoolers believe lying is bad, but children as young as 3 sometimes tell white lies to protect others' feelings.

There are two main types of lies that concern parents:

● **Self-protective lies** involve children trying to get themselves out of trouble or avoid punishment after they've done something wrong. These include denying a misdeed or blaming someone else.

● **Wishful thinking lies** involve bragging or falsely claiming something they want to happen is true. For instance, it's common for 6-year-olds to say Mommy is pregnant when she's not.

" "

THE BEST WAY TO DEAL WITH YOUR CHILD'S LYING IS TO MAKE IT EASY FOR HIM TO TELL THE TRUTH.

SEE RELATED TOPICS
But I didn't hear you: pp.112–113
She's not listening: pp.146–147

THE ROUTE TO FOLLOW

Addressing a lie

SELF-PROTECTIVE LIES

DESCRIPTION

Parents are only about 60 percent accurate at detecting lies their kids tell denying misbehavior.

Even 3-year-olds can mask nonverbal signs that they're lying, by smiling and making eye contact.

Preschoolers' false stories fall apart when questioned.

TRIGGERS

Fear of getting in trouble.

Breaking a rule.

Wanting to get someone else in trouble.

Trying to avoid blame for something he has done wrong.

RESPONSE

1. **Set the stage for honesty.** Tell your child he won't get in trouble and you'll be pleased if he tells the truth about misbehavior.

2. **Don't ask "Did you do it?" questions.** Demanding an admission of guilt encourages kids to lie.

3. **Read stories about honesty.** Inspiring tales, such as George Washington admitting to chopping the cherry tree, work better than cautionary tales, such as "The Boy Who Cried Wolf," to encourage truth telling.

4. **Let him try again.** Ask, "Is that the whole truth or part of the truth, did you get confused, or did you forget?" to allow him to shift his story to the truth.

5. **Don't discipline too harshly.** Heavy consequences make kids afraid to tell the truth.

WISHFUL THINKING LIES

DESCRIPTION

Occupy a murky space between belief and imagination.

Examples: Saying that you own a pony (when you don't), that he's able to ride a bike (when he can't), or that he already went potty (when he didn't).

Other parents may ask you about these tall tales.

TRIGGERS

Believing that wishing can magically make something happen.

Wanting to impress others or feel "big."

Wanting to avoid the inconvenience of adults' rules, for example, lying about completing homework to go out to play.

RESPONSE

1. **Acknowledge the wish.** Say, "You wish that would happen" or "You wish you could do that."

2. **Clarify.** Smile and ask, "Did that really happen, or is it your imagination?" Explain that if he tells you it's his imagination, you can enjoy imagining it with him.

3. **Give him the words.** Teach him to say, "Wouldn't it be fun if…" to let people know when he's playing with his imagination, so they're not confused.

4. **Trust but verify.** If you think your child might be lying to avoid a task, ask, "Should I check that you did it, or do you want to try again?"

5. **Model honesty.** If your child hears you exaggerating or making up excuses, he'll learn that it's socially acceptable to do so.

"I had an accident."

Even if your child is mainly dry during the day, there may be times when she still wets her pants. Daytime wetting affects about 1 in 7 children aged 4 but reduces to 1 in 75 over the age of 5. It may happen only during the day or along with bed-wetting.

SCENARIO | **Your child keeps wetting her pants during the day.**

SHE SAYS

"I had an accident."

Children need to urinate between four and seven times a day. If your child has been dry before, there could be a physical reason for her accidents, such as a urinary tract infection, which means she is peeing in smaller but more frequent amounts.

I didn't do it: pp.142–143
I wet the bed: pp.158–159

MOST CHILDREN WILL HAVE ACCIDENTS. SHARE YOUR CONFIDENCE THAT PRETTY SOON SHE'LL BE ABLE TO STAY DRY.

YOU MIGHT THINK

"She knows how to stay dry. Why is she still having accidents?"

WHAT SHE'S THINKING

"There's so much to do, I just forget to go to the bathroom."

You may be annoyed that she didn't take herself to the bathroom in time, but accidents are common at this age. Don't put her back in pull-ups or diapers because that could make her feel babyish or ashamed.

Your child may delay going to the bathroom because she's enjoying playing. She may also leave it too late because she feels self-conscious about going, dislikes bathroom smells, or is afraid of getting locked in.

HOW TO RESPOND

In the moment...

Stay positive. Express delight when she uses the toilet and just clean up matter-of-factly if she has an accident. She'll soon learn it's easier to stay dry.

Consider the cause. Sometimes an increase in accidents is a sign of stress. Have there been recent changes in your family? Is your child avoiding something? She may need extra support from you.

In the long term...

Take bathroom breaks. Make trips to the bathroom part of your daily routine. Tell your child she just has to "check" whether there's pee ready to come out.

Help her slow down. Get her to take her time when she pees. This will help the faucetlike muscle—the sphincter—at the base of the bladder open fully to empty completely.

Get your child to drink more. Rather than getting your child to drink less, encourage her to drink six to eight glasses of water-based drinks throughout the day so her bladder fills properly and sends stronger signals that it needs to be emptied.

"She's not listening."

At this age, your child is beginning to move beyond parallel play—playing side by side—to cooperating with his playmates around a shared focus. While he is still learning to do this, conflicts with peers may be more frequent.

SCENARIO | **While playing in a sandbox, your child pushes his friend in a fight over how they should play.**

HE SAYS

"She's not listening."

YOU MIGHT THINK

"Why is he being mean? No one will want to play with him if he's too rough."

Parents want their children to play nicely. But it's baffling and frustrating for kids when playmates don't want to do things their way. Most children this age will sometimes use force to get what they want. Studies show that boys and girls may hit, push, grab, or use other physical strategies to try to make the game go their way.

You may feel embarrassed if your child acts aggressively toward a peer, especially if other adults are present. But if no one is getting hurt, don't leap to intervene. Tiffs are usually quickly forgotten if both kids want to continue their game.

CHILDREN CAN TEACH EACH OTHER HOW TO GET ALONG. WITH LOTS OF PLAYTIME, THEY MOSTLY LEARN TO WORK IT OUT.

WHAT HE'S THINKING

"I'm so frustrated that she's not doing what I want her to do!"

At this age, compromise, sharing, and taking turns are difficult for children. Your child's frustration when things don't go his way can bubble over into using physical force to impose his will on his peers.

HOW TO RESPOND

In the moment...

Stand back and observe. If the children are arguing, pushing, or grabbing without too much force, just watch. Step in only if someone will get hurt or something will get broken. If they were having fun, children are often motivated to come up with a solution for themselves.

Point out the cues. Some children have trouble picking up on others' reactions. Instead of scolding your child, help him see his friend's response. Say, "She looks mad. I don't think she liked it when you took the shovel from her. What can you do to make it better?"

Don't play referee. Your child may demand that you make the other child do things his way. Instead, reframe the dilemma around fairness: "You want to do it one way. She wants to do it another way. What would be fair to both of you?"

In the long term...

Role-play social skills. Help your child practice asking politely, sharing, cooperating, or taking turns. Remind him just before entering a social situation so these skills are top of mind when he needs them.

Take it outside. Children often have more fun and squabble less when they play outdoors. Fresh air and room to move tend to make kids calmer and more agreeable.

SEE RELATED TOPICS

I'm telling: pp.120–121
You can't come to my party: pp.152–153

"I don't want to clean up."

Play is key to your child's emotional and intellectual development. The downside of play at this age is the trail of puzzle pieces, LEGO bricks, play figures, and crayons that are left behind. Your child may need help to learn how to help clean up.

SCENARIO | The living room floor is littered with toys, but your child does nothing when you ask her to help put them away.

SHE SAYS

"I don't want to clean up."

When your child is absorbed in playing, it makes sense for her to have all her playthings spread out but still within easy reach. Then, she can stretch her imagination and create new games by using them together—making a house out of bricks for her play figures and animals, for instance.

YOU MIGHT THINK

"The constant mess is annoying. Why does she pull everything out instead of playing with one toy at a time?"

While you may prefer more order and less chaos at home, your child doesn't see the "mess" as annoying. Most adults like to have "homes" for things to be put away. Your child will need to learn this over time.

SEE RELATED TOPICS
Look what I did!: pp.92–93
I don't want to: pp.156–157

HOW TO RESPOND

In the moment...

Join in. Cleaning up all her toys alone will feel overwhelming to your child at this age. So offer to help by saying, "Let's do it together!"

Give guidance. Instead of saying "clean up," give her a specific job. Say, "Please put all the dinosaurs into their box," or ask her to pick up her blue blocks while you pick up the red ones.

Make cleaning up part of the fun. Invent a special cleaning up song or choose an up-tempo playlist as an energetic backing track. Or set the kitchen timer to challenge her to race to see who can put the most LEGO bricks back in their box and be Cleaning Up Champion today.

In the long term...

Cut the clutter. If children have a large number of toys and no place to put them, cleaning up can seem too daunting. Consider reducing the number of toys your child has out to 10 or fewer and have easy-to-use clear storage boxes or shelves for each. Put away extra toys and rotate them in occasionally for novelty.

Make it regular. Schedule clean-up time at the same time every day—perhaps the interval just before dinner—to get kids into the habit.

WHAT SHE'S THINKING

"If I put away my toys, I might not find them again or remember how I set them out."

To your child, being told to clean up may feel like she is being asked to break up the world she has just created. It can also seem overwhelming if she has a lot of toys out.

A FAMILY HOME IS NOT A SHOW HOUSE. IF YOUR CHILD IS HELPING TO MAKE IT LESS MESSY, YOU'RE ON THE RIGHT PATH.

"You have to."

If your child is very verbal and full of ideas, he may try to order playmates around. But his bossy behavior can drive other children away. Research finds that being able to play collaboratively is key for making and keeping friends.

SCENARIO | **On a playdate, you overhear your child telling his friend he must play the game by his rules.**

HE SAYS

"You have to."

Children frequently hear grown-ups telling them what to do. So, when a playmate tries to take charge, they find it very irritating, so they insist, "You're not the boss of me!" then argue or just walk away.

SEE RELATED TOPICS

I'm telling: pp.120–121
She's not listening: pp.146–147

YOU MIGHT THINK

"I want him to stand up for himself, but if he keeps being bossy, he won't have any friends."

WHAT HE'S THINKING

"My way is the right way!"

There is a big difference between leadership, which involves making others want to follow, and bossiness, which means telling others what to do. Your child needs to learn how to communicate his ideas in ways that others will want to hear.

Your child is convinced that he's right and willing to resort to demands or even threats to get his way. He's so focused on his idea of how things should be that he may be blind to other children's reactions to his bossiness.

HOW TO RESPOND

In the moment...

Shift the action. If the other child is sulking, arguing, or complaining about getting bossed around, that could mean your child is pushing too hard. End the stalemate by suggesting a snack or taking them outside (or inside).

Have a quiet word. If his bossy behavior is ruining the playdate, take your child aside and point out how the other child might be feeling. Suggest that he ask what his playmate would like to do.

In the long term...

Encourage flexibility. Explain that being flexible means being able to bend by cooperating, compromising or accepting a less-than-perfect option. It's a kind thing to do. Notice and thank him when he's flexible.

Watch his words. Tell your child to avoid saying words like "You have to" or "You can't." Agree on a secret signal—such as a throat-clearing "ahem"—to remind him to change directions by saying, "Okay," "What do you want to do?" "How about...?" or "Please."

Model polite requests. When you give directions with a smile, a please, and a calm voice, your child begins to learn that this is how people ask for what they want.

"You can't come to my party."

Your child is now starting to make closer friendships and form social groups, but it's hard for her to manage conflicts. Birthday parties can be opportunities for her to wield social power to include or exclude others.

SCENARIO | You overhear your child telling a classmate that she's not invited to her birthday party.

SHE SAYS

"You can't come to my party."

YOU MIGHT THINK

"Why is she being so mean? I don't want her to be seen as a bully."

At this age, children are just grasping that other kids can have different thoughts and feelings. They feel frustrated when peers don't do what they want. The threat of no birthday invitation (even if it's months away!) is a clumsy attempt to get her way.

Children are still learning empathy. Unless you point it out, she won't realize that her words can be just as painful as hitting. She's not trying to be cruel; she's experimenting with social power to try to get peers to do what she wants.

MODEL KINDNESS TO OTHERS. EXPLAIN HOW CRUEL WORDS CAN HURT AS MUCH AS HITTING.

WHAT SHE'S THINKING

"It's my party, and I'm in charge. I decide who should be there."

Your child is still working out her place in the classroom social pecking order. She knows other children want to go to parties and that, as the birthday girl, she has some say about who is on the guest list. Unless she learns she is being unkind, she will use this fact to try to control her social world.

HOW TO RESPOND

In the moment...

Ask her reasons. Out of the hearing of other children, ask why she doesn't want to invite this classmate. She may need your guidance to resolve a conflict, cope with jealousy, or handle a social dilemma.

Point out the hurt. Tell your child to imagine what it would feel like if someone told her in front of others that she wasn't invited to a party. Would she feel sad? Angry? Left out? Help her understand that unkind words can hurt others.

In the long term...

Insist on kindness. Although your child has some say about the guest list, don't allow her to be cruel by, for example, inviting all but one girl in her class. Either invite everyone or ask just a few close friends. Give invitations discreetly, outside school, so no one feels rejected.

Teach conflict resolution. Use role-play to help your child learn better ways to solve conflicts with classmates, such as asking nicely for what she wants, taking turns, or taking a short break from playing together.

Play it cool. Birthday parties matter to young children, but if the buildup is too intense, your child will likely be bossy with peers and disappointed when the event doesn't match the hype.

SEE RELATED TOPICS
I didn't do it: pp.142–143
She's not listening: pp.146–147

Birthday parties

What used to be simple affairs—built around musical chairs, cake, and ice cream—birthday parties have become more elaborate events. But birthday parties don't have to be expensive to be fun.

Your child's birthday is a significant date in your family's calendar—and the reason for a party to celebrate. As the date approaches, it's helpful to talk to your child about the true meaning of birthdays.

Because of the simple way young children see cause and effect, research has found that before the age of 6, almost half of young children believe it's having a party on the birthday itself that makes them a year older. They don't understand that their birthday marks the passing of a whole year. So explain that it's not the party that makes them older but the days that have passed and what they have learned.

Looking over photos from the past year can be a fun way for children to see how much they've grown and learned.

In terms of length of parties, aim for 1–2 hours depending on your child's age.

1

Have a pre-party chat.
From the age of 4 or so, children may want a party based on a favorite TV show, book, or movie. Don't choose a theme too far in advance, though, since their interests may change.

4

Pick your time.
Choose the window when your child is at his most alert and even-tempered; it's best to work around nap times for younger children.

7

Do it your child's way.
Birthday parties are designed to make the birthday girl or birthday boy feel special. The best way to do that is to organize a party that's just for your child. You want to plan around his wishes and his interests, not those of others.

❝ ❞

YOUNG CHILDREN WILL ENJOY A PARTY MUCH MORE IF IT'S PITCHED AT JUST THE RIGHT DEVELOPMENTAL LEVEL FOR THEM.

GOOD PRACTICE

10 key principles

2
Consider the guest list.
To decide how many guests would make the party fun and enjoyable for your child, follow the "age plus one" rule. Though once children start school, that may have to bend somewhat.

3
Ask older children to be sensitive.
If your child does not want to invite everyone in his class, ask him to be sensitive by not talking about his party in front of those who are not invited. But don't let him exclude only one boy or girl.

5
Prepare for meltdowns.
Kids tend to have fewer conflicts with peers when they play outside. Invite friends (plus families) to a picnic in a park. Too many children inside can be overwhelming for young children.

6
Ask parents to help.
Children aren't always ready to separate from their parents during social events. On the invite, be clear about whether you want parents and siblings to stay.

8
Leave present opening for afterward.
Until the age of 3, some children may not understand that they have to leave the gifts they've brought with them and can't take them home. Collect presents on arrival so that they don't distract from the fun.

9
Help him be a good host.
Encourage your child to greet every guest, make sure everyone is included, and thank the guests when they leave.

10
Stay grounded.
If you recall your own childhood parties, you may remember the best moments were about the fun you had with your friends, not the venue or how much money the party cost.

2–3
YEARS OLD

Stagger gifts
Give your child a few presents to open after the event, but hold back others to give throughout the year.

Keep it simple
A single activity is easiest for 2-year-olds—water, sand, or modeling clay—to meet their need for parallel play. But by 3, children are ready for circle activity games.

4–5
YEARS OLD

Avoid school class dilemmas
Either ask a small group that is less than half of the class or ask the whole class. And have plenty of group games prepared.

Go ballistic!
Kids this age love balloons because they float and move slowly, allowing them to manipulate them better.

6–7
YEARS OLD

Invite VIPs only
As peer groups become more important, your child will want more say in the theme and who's on the guest list.

Choose a favorite activity
Children now prefer parties based on their favorite activities and sharing these with their friends—popular choices are soccer, swimming, dancing, or art.

"I don't want to!"

Your child has strong feelings, and sometimes she may have trouble managing them or communicating them peacefully. She may even lash out physically. Intellectually, she knows better, but in the heat of the moment, she may do things she later regrets.

SCENARIO | Your child kicks out at you when you tell her it's time to stop watching TV and come upstairs for a bath.

SHE SAYS

"I don't want to!"

YOU MIGHT THINK

"I'm shocked. How could she hurt me like this?"

Kicking, hitting, and biting are undesirable but not uncommon child behaviors, even at this age. Your child wants to do things her way, and she may resist your directions. If she's upset, she may express her resistance aggressively. She's not intentionally hurting you; she just wants her way.

It's almost impossible to stay calm when you're physically hurt. Say, "Ow! That hurt!" but resist the temptation to grab or hurt your child back. If you're injured or very upset, remove yourself from the situation until you're calmer, but be sure kicking doesn't work to get your child what she wants.

THE BEST TIME TO TALK ABOUT PHYSICAL AGGRESSION IS NOT IN THE HEAT OF THE MOMENT.

WHAT SHE'S THINKING

"I didn't mean to kick Mommy. It just happened!"

Almost as soon as your child kicked you, she probably regretted it. She may be shocked that she's capable of hurting you. However, her guilt may make her defensive and cause her to blame you for her outburst. She needs your help to learn better ways to handle frustration.

SEE RELATED TOPICS
It's not fair!: pp.180–181
But I'm not tired: pp.216–217

HOW TO RESPOND

In the moment...

Don't escalate. If you respond to your child kicking you by yelling, grabbing, or trying to hurt her back, the situation will get very ugly, very fast. You can't help your child regain self-control if you are acting out of control. Step farther away instead of moving closer. Talk softly, rather than yelling. Repeat your direction with calm certainty, "It's time to go upstairs."

Wait to talk it through. When you've both calmed down, then you can talk about the kicking. Start by acknowledging your child's feelings. "You were mad when I asked you to come upstairs." Your understanding makes it easier for her to unbend. Listen to her view then remind her, "It's never okay to kick anyone."

Regain your bond. After you've discussed the incident, let your child know that you've forgiven her by doing a small kindness for her—unrelated to the kicking issue. Give her a cuddle, or make a favorite meal to show that you still love her and you've moved on.

In the long term...

Problem solve together. Ask your child, "How can we prevent this from happening again?" Maybe she could use her words to tell you what she wants or needs. Maybe you could give her a warning. Maybe you both could compromise somehow.

Look for triggers. Pay attention to when your child lashes out so you can try to prevent these incidents. Being tired, hungry, or overstimulated can interfere with self-control. Routines help your child know what to expect. Polite requests are easier for her to listen to than harsh orders.

"I wet the bed."

Staying dry through the night is the last stage of toilet training. It takes many types of development to come together for this to happen, so children reach this point at different ages. Four out of ten 4-year-olds and a quarter of 5-year-olds wet the bed.

SCENARIO | **Your child has wet the bed for the third time this week.**

HE SAYS

"I wet the bed."

There are many reasons your child may be wetting the bed. His nervous system may not yet be wired well enough for his bladder to send a wake-up call to his brain, or he may have a smaller bladder. If you or your partner wet the bed in childhood, he has a 25 percent higher risk of doing the same.

" "

TRUST THAT YOUR CHILD WILL GET THERE. HELP HIM KEEP HIS SELF-CONFIDENCE INTACT WHILE HE LEARNS TO BE DRY AT NIGHT.

YOU MIGHT THINK

"It's exhausting to change the bed in the middle of the night. When is he going to grow out of this?"

Despite your frustrations, try to be understanding. Knowing that most kids grow out of wetting the bed is little comfort when nights are broken and there's extra washing, but bed-wetting is out of your child's control so be supportive.

SEE RELATED TOPICS
I had a bad dream: pp.140–141
I had an accident: pp.144–145

WHAT HE'S THINKING

"I feel ashamed. I don't want anyone else to know."

Bed-wetting can dent your child's self-worth—he may believe it's babyish and feel ashamed of the upset it causes. He'll need plenty of comfort, one-on-one time, and reassurance that he'll grow out of it. Anxiety can also trigger bed-wetting.

HOW TO RESPOND

In the moment...

Stay upbeat. Praise your child for his dry nights. Be matter of fact about his wet ones. All you need to say is: "Let's get you up and change these sheets."

Give him a positive mind-set. While making his bed, talk to him about being "dry" and "not dry" rather than being "wet," which may trigger feelings of shame. If you or your partner wet the bed as children, let him know because he will see that you've grown out of it.

In the long term...

Address the practicalities. Keep a regular bedtime routine. Don't let him drink too much in the hour before bed, and take him to the toilet just before he goes to sleep. Make it easy for him to get to the bathroom during the night. Consider using pull-ups if bedwetting is frequent until he is dry most nights.

Talk to him. See if you can discover any emotional causes of his bed-wetting. Is he worried about something that could have triggered these episodes?

Seek advice. While most children grow out of bed-wetting by the age of 6 or 7, if it happens a lot, keep a diary and see your GP to rule out any physical causes.

"Will bad people hurt us?"

As they get older, children are exposed to much more information about the world and its risks. Your child may overhear older children or grown-ups talk about terrorist attacks, leading to anxiety that "bad people" may want to harm her and the people she loves, too.

SCENARIO | After a terrorist attack, your child is worried about such events happening to her or anyone she knows.

SHE SAYS

"Will bad people hurt us?"

YOU MIGHT THINK

"How do I comfort her when I'm feeling sad and scared, too?"

Children see the world in black-and-white terms—your child wants to believe that bad things happen only to bad people. So it's shocking for her to discover that such events can happen to regular people. She will be picking up on anxious faces and take it to mean there's something to worry about.

Hearing about a terror attack in which innocent people have died has upset your child's sense of security—and maybe your own, too. You can't guarantee that nothing bad will ever happen, but you can tell your child, "My number-one job is to keep you safe."

SEE RELATED TOPICS

I'm scared of the dark: pp.118–119
Why did Grandpa die?: pp.166–167

CHILDREN TAKE THEIR CUE FROM YOU. RATIONALIZE YOUR OWN FEARS SO YOU CAN REASSURE YOUR CHILD.

WHAT SHE'S THINKING

"Am I safe? Are we safe?"

At this age, her world is split starkly into "good guys" and "bad guys." So it's reassuring for her to discover that there are far more good guys working to keep her safe. In fact, making herself feel safe "right now" is top of her list of priorities until she regains her previous balance of belief about safety in the world.

HOW TO RESPOND

In the moment...

Listen to her. Ask her what she knows and what she feels. Finding out what your child has heard and asking her to name her fears will help you to keep your answer simple and target her specific concerns.

Make a list. Or draw a picture of all the people who are working to keep your child safe. This could include relatives, friends, neighbors, teachers, the police, the army, and so on.

Give extra hugs. Hug your child now and give more hugs than usual; focus on talking about the positives in life, which will reassure her that the world is a safe place.

Help her feel that she can protect herself. Your child feels that her security is out of her hands. So talk about the small ways she already keeps herself safe—using a seat belt in the car and wearing a helmet when she rides her bike, for example.

In the long term...

Limit exposure to on-screen news.
Your child does not yet realize that every repeated news clip is not a new incident. It's best not to expose her to such images because she can't yet put them in context.

"It feels good."

Children are curious, and one of the first things they want to learn about is their bodies. When they find their genitals, they discover that touching these areas feels more pleasurable than other body parts, so some children may touch them repeatedly.

SCENARIO | **While watching a movie together, you notice your child has one hand down his pants.**

HE SAYS

"It feels good."

Just as babies discover their fingers, toes, and belly buttons in their first year, as kids get older, they will also discover their genitals. As your child's hand coordination improves, he may get into a habit of enjoying these pleasurable feelings as a way of entertaining or soothing himself.

" "

HOW YOU RESPOND TO SELF-TOUCHING CAN INFLUENCE WHETHER YOUR CHILD GROWS UP FEELING PROUD OF OR ASHAMED OF HIS BODY.

YOU MIGHT THINK

"I feel uncomfortable seeing him rubbing his genitals. What if he does it in front of others?"

Touching their genitals for comfort or pleasure is normal and common behavior for children that peaks around age 5. It decreases in frequency as children get older and become more aware of social norms.

SEE RELATED TOPICS
I want a cuddle: pp.90–91
I'm scared of the dark: pp.118–119

WHAT HE'S THINKING

"I like touching this part of my body. It feels good—and different from touching other parts of me."

Self-touching is a soothing activity, much like sucking a thumb. Your child may touch himself more when he's bored, sleepy, or tense. He finds self-touching distracting, pleasurable, and comforting. It has not yet become associated with adult sexual activity.

HOW TO RESPOND

In the moment...

Use distraction and redirection. When your child is very young, distracting him with a book, toy, or fun activity is the easiest way to stop self-touching while around others. When he gets to about age 5, you can explain that this is a private activity, reserved for when he's alone.

Help him find other ways to self-soothe. Pay attention to the feelings that might trigger self-touching. If he's bored, help him find something else to do. If he's anxious, reassurance or extra cuddling from you might help.

Stay neutral. Avoid saying "Stop it" or "That's bad," which could make him feel ashamed. If you make a fuss, he could do it more to get your attention. If he uses self-touching to fall asleep, ignore it.

In the long term...

Explain the science simply. If your son asks why his penis becomes harder sometimes, you can talk about how the body reacts in other ways. For example, show him how his pupils get bigger in dimmer light.

Rule out other causes. In about a third of cases, self-touching starts due to infection or irritated skin. Very rarely, self-touching interferes with daily functioning, is painful, or imitates adult sexual acts and could be related to exposure to inappropriate content or contact or a developmental disability. Consult your pediatrician if you're concerned.

"Was that good?"

Your child wants to please you. Your reactions contribute to helping her form her personal values and the standards she'll use to judge her actions. We never completely outgrow our wish for our parents to be proud of us. Help your child see herself through kind eyes.

SCENARIO | **In a game of tennis, your child hits the ball back twice in a row.**

GIVE FEEDBACK BUT BE PLEASABLE SO YOUR CHILD LEARNS TO JUDGE HERSELF KINDLY.

SHE SAYS

"Was that good?"

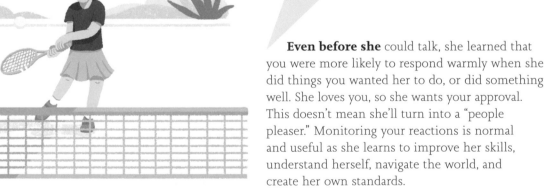

Even before she could talk, she learned that you were more likely to respond warmly when she did things you wanted her to do, or did something well. She loves you, so she wants your approval. This doesn't mean she'll turn into a "people pleaser." Monitoring your reactions is normal and useful as she learns to improve her skills, understand herself, navigate the world, and create her own standards.

SEE RELATED TOPICS
I do it!: pp.38–39
Look what I did!: pp.92–93

YOU MIGHT THINK

"I want my child to try hard, do well, and feel confident."

WHAT SHE'S THINKING

"I feel happy when Mommy and Daddy are pleased with me."

Your responses to her actions give her essential feedback about what is good or desirable behavior. Supportive, but not overblown, comments from you can help her recognize successes and keep trying in the face of frustration or failure.

Your child isn't able to feel proud of herself until age 6 or 7, but she recognizes when you're pleased long before that. As she grows, she'll take in feedback from others, but you're the start of building her self-esteem.

HOW TO RESPOND

In the moment...

Give useful feedback. Describe what she did right and how. Emphasize her effort or strategy rather than unchangeable qualities, so she understands how to continue to succeed. Research shows that even a simple thumbs up or high five can encourage kids to keep trying.

Be sincere, so your approval means something. Avoid too lavish "You're amazing!" praise because it feels false, encourages arrogance, or creates pressure. Also don't give empty praise for tasks that were easy for her.

Be pleasable. If your standards are too high, she'll feel hopeless and could give up trying to win your approval.

In the long term...

Help her see progress. Draw attention to how far she's come, so she feels hopeful about her ongoing learning and improvement. Don't compare her to others, or she'll feel dejected when she's not number one.

Enjoy her company. Show her your love doesn't have to be earned. Sometimes, just delight in her, without trying to teach or correct her.

"Why did Grandpa die?"

When someone dies, young children usually don't yet understand that death is final. They think it's temporary or that their loved one has gone to sleep. So it's useful to know how you can explain the situation sensitively while conveying the finality of this event.

SCENARIO | You have told your child that his grandpa has died.

HE SAYS

"Why did Grandpa die?"

YOU MIGHT THINK

"How do I explain death without scaring him?"

A death in the family will trigger lots of questions: "Why did Grandpa die? Where is he now? Can I play with him?" Giving clear, open, and honest information will put his mind at rest. At this age, children don't usually think about themselves dying.

Death is part of life, so you need to help your child understand when it touches his life. But since your child thinks literally, it's crucial that you use words that convey the finality of death. Avoid phrases such as "gone to sleep" or "we've lost him." It's important that you don't confuse him.

THOUGH YOUR INSTINCT MAY BE TO SHIELD YOUR CHILD, BEING OPEN IS BETTER THAN MAKING IT TABOO.

HOW TO RESPOND

In the moment...

Be open. Explain that when someone is dead, his body does not move; he can't eat, talk, breathe, or feel pain, and he doesn't wake up. Tell him everyone dies but you don't expect it to happen to you for a long time.

Give a reason. Explain simply why his grandpa died so he understands there's a reason his body stopped working: "Grandpa's heart wore out because he lived for so long."

Relate it to life. When explaining death to a child, it can help to link it to other experiences he knows, such as the death of a pet or a plant, so he understands its finality. If your family is religious, explain the customs and beliefs of your faith.

Ask him if he wants to draw his feelings. Because children tend to put themselves at the center of stories, they sometimes construct reasons they might be to blame. In his mind, your child might imagine: "Grandpa died because I didn't do what I was told." Ask him if wants to talk about, draw, or role-play how he feels so you understand his thinking better.

In the long term...

Give it time. Your child may want to talk about it for many months, so be prepared. Children also need tangible ways of mourning—going through family photos, making a keepsake box, releasing a balloon with his name on it, or planting a tree can help.

WHAT HE'S THINKING

"Are you going to die, too? Who will take care of me?"

Since your child may struggle with abstract concepts of time, such as "tomorrow" or "forever," it's hard for him to grasp that death is permanent and irreversible. This limited understanding is also reflected in how he experiences grief. Children go through "islands of grief"—sad one minute, happy the next.

SEE RELATED TOPICS

I feel sad: pp. 132–133
Will bad people hurt us?: pp. 160–161

"You promised."

Parents are their child's entire universe at this age—children learn to trust the world by trusting their parents. This means that when you make a commitment, it's important to stick to it, because children put so much faith in trusting that you will do what you say.

SCENARIO | **You said you would take your child to the park, but a work emergency means you can't go now.**

SHE SAYS

"You promised."

By now, your child is learning the rules adults expect her to follow, including keeping your promises. Her sense of fairness means she expects you to do the same. If you break your promise, she may get the message that your work is more important to you than she is.

SEE RELATED TOPICS
I love being with you: pp.108–109
You're always too busy: pp.128–129

YOU MIGHT THINK

"I wanted to take her, but that unexpected work emergency messed up our plans."

WHAT SHE'S THINKING

"Daddy said it, so it should have come true."

It's not always possible to stick to every promise if circumstances change. The look of disappointment on your child's face can be hard to bear. Explain what happened, but instead of defending or justifying your actions, focus on empathizing with your child's feelings.

Children this age tend to think their parents make all the decisions, so it's tricky for your child to grasp that someone else (your boss) can tell you what to do. If she can see that you're disappointed, too, and that it was beyond your control, then the damage can be repaired.

HOW TO RESPOND

In the moment...

Say sorry. Sympathize with your child's disappointment, and give her an unconditional apology. Tell her how important she is to you. Let her know that you're disappointed, too.

Let your child choose a fun alternative for now. Ask your child what she can do—coloring in a picture, for example—while you finish work. Then, tell her as soon as you're finished, you will do something special as planned.

In the long term...

Protect family time. You can't foresee all eventualities, but do prioritize time with your child; put your phone away when you can and turn off your email notifications.

Don't overpromise. Children have long and selective memories for things they particularly look forward to. Be careful about your wording, and don't use the word "promise" lightly. Instead, use phrases such as "I plan to…" or a "I am going to try" if there's any doubt at all.

Be sincere but don't go overboard begging for forgiveness. A change in plans is disappointing but bearable. If you overreact, your child will think, "Wow, I should be very upset about this."

Separation and divorce

Many families face the challenge of a separation or divorce. Whatever the reasons, it's difficult for everyone. For children, it can be very upsetting and confusing to see the two adults they love most go their separate ways.

Parental separation and divorce aren't merely events; they're evolving processes that touch on many aspects of a child's life.

Seeing less of one or both parents, going between homes with different rules, and dealing with changes in family finances or parental employment all add up to big adjustments for your child.

Research shows that it's not the split itself but the conflict between parents that hurts kids most. Although it can be hard to do when feelings are running high, respectfully communicating and cooperating with your ex is the best gift you can give your child to soften the impact of separation or divorce.

“ ”

WHEN ADULTS ARE CIVIL TO EACH OTHER AFTER A SEPARATION, CHILDREN COPE BETTER WITH ITS CHALLENGES.

1

Tell him together.
Most children will always remember being told about a separation. Present a united, optimistic front to make it a less painful memory.

4

Avoid buying treats out of guilt.
Your child might see them as a sign that you're trying to buy his cooperation or bribe him to bury his feelings.

7

Spare him the details.
You might be tempted to tell your child about upsetting things your ex did. Don't burden him with this info. Just say that you grew apart.

9

Be patient.
It can take at least two years for children and parents to feel settled emotionally after a split.

GOOD PRACTICE

10 key principles

2
Set out the basics.
Explain that you aren't happy together and have agreed to live apart. Tell him that you both will always love him, and nothing can change that.

3
Let him know what to expect.
Explain what will be the same or different in your child's life. Will he have to move or change schools? Answer his main concern, which is, "Who's going to look after me?" Tell him you both will, just in different places.

5
Don't bad-mouth your ex.
Whatever has gone on between you two adults, your child still loves and needs his other parent. Don't criticize your ex in front of your child, or the hostility can make him feel torn in two.

6
Accept your child's feelings.
Let him know it's normal to feel sad, mad, worried, relieved, or any mixture of feelings. When you decide to introduce a new romantic partner, wait until the relationship is serious and take it slowly. He might feel jealous of your new partner or disloyal to your ex.

8
Look after yourself.
Take care of yourself so you can support your child. Ask family and friends for help, or try support groups. If there are issues to be resolved with your ex, mediation can help avoid hostility.

10
Keep up routines.
Carry on with normal life as much as possible. Have rules, chores, playdates, and family get-togethers to help him see that the world is still safe and predictable. Ask your ex to keep the same bedtimes and mealtimes for consistency.

Age by age

2–3
YEARS OLD

Give lots of comfort
Children facing big events often erupt over small triggers because they have no coping reserves left. Respond to overwhelm with soothing.

Setbacks are normal
Children may regress— crying at bedtimes, wetting the bed, having separation anxiety. Be patient.

4–5
YEARS OLD

Tell the school
Let your child's teachers know so they can be understanding of any changes in behavior.

Be a united front
Be polite to your ex so your child doesn't feel awkward about having you both at events such as school assemblies and concerts.

6–7
YEARS OLD

Not their fault
Children this age may blame themselves for the split. Explain repeatedly that it wasn't his fault. Help him figure out what and how to tell friends.

Being realistic
Your child may fantasize about reconciliation, but this can hold back recovery and make it harder for him to accept when you move on. Tell him this is an adult decision he can't influence.

"I want it to be perfect."

Young children learn best by actively exploring and experimenting. A preoccupation with doing things "the right way" can get in the way of this. Guide your child toward being open to learning, not pursuing impossible perfection.

SCENARIO | **When your child realizes she has written an "S" backward in a birthday card, she rips it up.**

Research finds that perfectionism puts children at risk for anxiety, depression, and eating disorders. True perfectionism, in the form of harsh self-judgments and never feeling good enough, doesn't appear until the tween or teen years, but even 4-year-olds can show perfectionistic tendencies. Starting school may trigger unrealistic ideas of what they're supposed to be able to do.

Addressing two main issues can help your child avoid paralyzing perfectionism:

● **Overreacting to mistakes:** Young children have ideas about what they want a project to look like and may become very upset when the actual results don't resemble what's in their imagination.

● **Avoiding challenges:** Some children are reluctant to try new activities that they're not sure they can do perfectly. They anxiously hold themselves back from participating, especially if others are around to watch them.

TELL YOUR CHILD EVERYONE MAKES MISTAKES, AND WE CAN LEARN FROM THEM.

SEE RELATED TOPICS
I give up: pp.116–117
I'm the worst: pp.210–211

THE ROUTE TO FOLLOW

Addressing perfectionism

OVERREACTING TO MISTAKES

SIGNS

Crying or having a tantrum in response to small errors.

Saying that a project is completely ruined by a mistake.

Ripping up work that she feels isn't good enough.

Insisting that she has to start over when there's a flaw.

Resisting ideas on how to modify a project to incorporate an imperfection.

TRIGGERS

Artwork or projects that don't turn out the way she imagines them.

Wanting a gift she makes for someone to be just right.

Struggling with "big kid" school activities, such as trying to write letters or cutting with scissors.

RESPONSE

1. **Acknowledge her feelings.** Instead of arguing, say, "You're frustrated that it didn't turn out the way you wanted," so she knows you understand.

2. **Challenge all-or-nothing judgments.** Say, "There's one thing you don't like. Tell me three things you do like about your project."

3. **Model flexible thinking.** When you make a mistake, say, "It's not perfect, but it's good enough."

4. **Minimize pressure.** Avoid offering tips about how your child could make her projects "even better."

5. **Tolerate her made-up rules, when possible.** It's common for kids to want their toys arranged a certain way or to refuse an imperfect apple. Most outgrow this insistence on things being "just right."

AVOIDING CHALLENGES

SIGNS

Refusing to do activities that she isn't instantly good at.

Claiming that she's bad at some skill and will never be able to learn to do it.

Giving up quickly if she struggles.

Feeling very anxious about situations where people might watch her doing something.

TRIGGERS

School concerts or other performance situations.

Seeing older siblings or peers easily do something she hasn't yet learned to do.

New situations where she's unsure of what she's supposed to do or if she can do it.

RESPONSE

1. **Break it down.** Help her master small steps before moving to bigger ones. Say she hasn't learned it yet.

2. **Normalize struggle.** Tell her struggling is a sign her brain is growing. Encourage her to be a doer of hard things. Explain that it takes a while to learn most skills.

3. **Notice and appreciate qualities** that can't be measured, such as kindness, curiosity, and humor.

4. **Focus on process.** Comment on her effort, strategy, persistence, and enjoyment. Explain that you enjoy watching her, no matter what or how she does.

5. **Help her see progress.** Point out how she kept trying and became more capable. Skills that were difficult before are now much easier for her.

"No coloring on the wall."

Even though children are learning lots of rules at this age, it doesn't always mean they follow them every time. As they test boundaries and learn to control their impulses to stop themselves from doing the first thing that comes into their heads, rules will be broken.

SCENARIO | You catch your child drawing on the wall, as he cheerfully repeats the rule he's breaking.

HE SAYS

"No coloring on the wall."

YOU MIGHT THINK

"He knows he shouldn't draw on walls. Why is he doing it?"

Your child may view this drawing as an "accident" because he wasn't trying to be bad when he held a crayon and then saw the wall—like a giant sheet of paper. He knows the rules but doesn't really understand the reasons behind them. He can tell when you're mad but isn't always good at anticipating your reactions.

When temptation is high, your child's impulses may push past his wish to please you. Such rule breaking is not defiance. He's conflicted—the areas of his brain that govern self-control are still being constructed, so his urge to create has overpowered his ability to follow the rules.

SEE RELATED TOPICS
I didn't do it: pp.142–143
Was that good?: pp.164–165

" "

JUST BECAUSE CHILDREN KNOW A RULE DOESN'T MEAN THEY CAN ALWAYS CONTROL THEIR BEHAVIOR ENOUGH TO FOLLOW IT.

WHAT HE'S THINKING

"I love the way I can move my crayon along the wall as I draw."

Your child is eager to make his mark on his world, and writing on that big wall seems exciting! At this stage of developing hand–eye control, he also finds it much easier to scribble on a vertical surface than a flat one.

HOW TO RESPOND

In the moment...

(1)

Understand his struggle. If your child repeats back the rule when you catch him red-handed, don't be exasperated. He's trying to show you that he knows the rule and wishes he could follow it. He can't explain why his impulses got the better of him.

(2)

Ask him to help. Reinforce the rule and guide him back to good behavior by having him help clean off his drawing.

(3)

Explain what's appropriate. Redirect your child's creative impulses by telling him what he should do, rather than emphasizing what he shouldn't do. Say, "We draw only on paper." Then have him do that.

In the long term...

Provide other opportunities. Help meet his need to draw on a larger scale by buying rolls of paper to use on a vertical easel or use outdoor chalk to make the most of big spaces outside.

Encourage his art sessions. Drawing is one of the most important ways young children can express their thoughts and feelings, as well as develop motor skills. Hold back on showing your artistic talents, which may make your child frustrated because he will feel he cannot match them. Instead, be interested but let him decide what goes in his picture.

CHAPTER 5

6–7
YEARS OLD

"I have to tell you something!"

Children live almost completely in the present until they are about 7. They tend to interrupt adults when they are talking, because they are so focused on their own needs. Learning to wait takes time and practice.

SCENARIO | **You're on the phone to a friend, and your child constantly interrupts you to tell you about a new game she's invented.**

SHE SAYS

"I have to tell you something!"

YOU MIGHT THINK

"Why does she always interrupt me as soon as I get on the phone?"

Your child is sensitive to where your attention is. When she sees you engaged with something that doesn't involve her, she may suddenly feel the need to get your attention.

Your child's growing independence means that she doesn't need your constant attention, but she's still young enough that when she gets the idea of wanting your attention, she wants it now! She needs your help to develop the ability to delay gratification.

HELP YOUR CHILD UNDERSTAND THAT EVEN IF YOU ARE BUSY, YOU ARE ALWAYS INTERESTED IN HER.

HOW TO RESPOND

In the moment...

①

Give her a signal. Acknowledge that she is there— give her a smile and squeeze her hand to say that you've noticed she wants something. You could also put your fingers up to show how many minutes you expect to be.

②

Give a time frame. To avoid her thinking it will be ages until you come back to her, say: "I will need about 10 minutes of quiet time on the phone to Jane, and as soon as I'm finished, I can listen to you." Setting a timer might help her wait. Keep your word when the time's up.

In the long term...

Schedule calls for child-free times. As much as possible, plan long phone calls—or ask friends to call back—when your child is at school or in bed. This will minimize frustration for both of you and allow you to enjoy each other's company.

Plan ahead. Prevention is the best way to head off interruptions. Prepare some toys, books, or other quiet activities for when you are on the phone. If the phone rings, ask your daughter: "Is there anything you need before I start talking? How will you keep yourself busy?"

Set a good example. Adults often forget that they interrupt children, too. Be polite and respectful if you want your child to do the same. For example, tell her: "It looks like you're having a great time playing that game. But I need to interrupt you in 2 minutes to clean up before bedtime."

WHAT SHE'S THINKING

"I can't wait. I really, really, really want to tell Mommy right now!"

By this age, your child is able to wait for short periods of time, but it's difficult. Keep the wait short and offer reassurance and coping strategies to help her tolerate the delay.

SEE RELATED TOPICS
Carving out quality time: pp.84–85
I'm bored: pp.218–219

"It's not fair!"

As their sense of fairness develops, children may start to complain a lot if they feel they are being treated unjustly, especially compared to siblings. This behavior marks the beginning of understanding justice, but it's still very much self-centered.

SCENARIO | **Your child asks why he has to go to bed an hour earlier than his 9-year-old sister.**

HE SAYS

"It's not fair!"

YOU MIGHT THINK

"He doesn't understand that she's older."

It's hard for your child to leave a situation when he feels like all sorts of exciting things could be happening in his absence. He may be overreacting about having to go upstairs earlier because this is not really about bedtime but more about how much time he spends with you.

It's exasperating that children are always on the lookout for the slightest sign of unequal treatment, because they hate to miss out. As they get older, they'll understand that fair doesn't always mean equal. Avoid countering with the remark, "Life isn't fair." Although true, it's too big a concept for now.

" "

BY GIVING HIM "SPECIAL TIME" EACH DAY, HE IS LESS LIKELY TO CLAIM THAT HE IS BEING TREATED UNFAIRLY AT OTHER TIMES.

WHAT HE'S THINKING

"She always gets what she wants."

Children this age are super-vigilant about getting the same amount of time, attention, perks, and treats as siblings; however, your child might overlook the times when he gets the better deal. He just doesn't want to miss out on anything.

HOW TO RESPOND

In the moment...

Stop and listen. Offer a hug and say, "It's hard to be the first one to go to bed" or "You hate feeling left out when everyone is still up and you have to go to bed."

Offer hope. Different children have different needs at different ages. In the case of a 6-year-old and a 9-year-old, the younger child needs more sleep for his faster-growing brain to develop. Tell him that when he is 9, he will be allowed to stay up later, too.

Sidestep a debate. Offer to take him to bed to read a story of his choice—so he feels that he has got back some control over the situation—and say that you will be happy to talk about bedtime rules tomorrow.

In the long term...

Give him special time. Set aside 10–15 minutes of one-on-one time with him each day, on top of bedtime story time. Some extra one-on-one attention from you could help lessen your child's focus on fairness. Do something you both enjoy together on a regular basis.

Explain how "fair" is not always "identical." To illustrate that children need different things, give him other scenarios. For example, if his sister likes books about hamsters and he doesn't, should they both get the same books for their birthdays?

SEE RELATED TOPICS
But Mommy said I could: pp.186–187
But I'm not tired: pp.216–217

"I can't do it."

We all want our children to be confident, eager learners, so when your child's anxieties about her abilities make her think it's not worth trying, she'll need your help to cope with self-doubt and embrace the idea that "I can't do it" comes with a "yet."

SCENARIO | After barely starting her English homework, your child crumples up her worksheet and throws it on the floor.

SHE SAYS

"I can't do it."

YOU MIGHT THINK

"Why does she give up so easily?"

Your child feels anxious that she does not know what to write. This anxiety has triggered the fight-or-flight response in her brain, which means the rational part stops working, and she really cannot work out how to tackle the task.

You may feel frustrated or worried that your child tends to give up if she's not instantly successful. Your first instinct will likely be to give her a pep talk and tell her she can do it, but she won't believe you because your words do not match her feelings.

TO BELIEVE IT, CHILDREN NEED MANY EXPERIENCES SHOWING THAT EFFORT LEADS TO PROGRESS.

WHAT SHE'S THINKING

"I feel stuck. That means I'm not good at this, so I give up."

It takes courage to keep trying with difficult tasks. Your child hasn't yet learned that feeling stuck is temporary. She interprets her struggle as a sign that she lacks ability, so she feels hopeless. She needs your support to persevere past self-doubt.

SEE RELATED TOPICS
I'm the worst: pp.210–211
I'm not as good as them: pp.220–221

HOW TO RESPOND
In the moment...

Put feelings in context. Empathize but make it clear that her feelings don't apply to everything, for all time. Say, "You're feeling frustrated right now" or "You're struggling with this assignment" or "Your confused because you haven't learned this yet."

Tell her she can choose not to listen. Negative self-talk is a form of internal bullying. Encourage her to imagine a character in her head who tells her she can't do her work and give it a name, such as "Miss Can't" or "Miss Negative," so she can tell it to keep quiet.

Find baby steps. Help your child find a strategy for approaching the task. Break it down into small, doable steps so your child can build momentum and gain confidence that she can handle it. If the task truly is beyond her, find one part that she can do then write a note explaining where and how she's struggling so the teacher can help.

In the long term...

Reframe struggle as a sign her brain is growing. Explain to her that just like a muscle gets stronger by doing difficult work, her brain does, too. Be careful not to help more than she needs, or she'll lose the opportunity to learn.

Tell stories. Remind her about times when she struggled and then triumphed, so she realizes that the struggle is temporary. For instance, "I remember when you were first learning to swim. You were afraid to put your face in the water, but now you're practically a fish!"

"I hate you!"

Children have more extremes of emotions than adults. So while your child adores you when he is happy, when things don't go his way, he feels everything is terrible, including you. In that moment, he may interpret his frustration as hatred.

SCENARIO | **You won't let your child watch one more episode of his favorite TV show.**

HE SAYS

"I hate you!"

YOU MIGHT THINK

"How could he say that? Does he mean it?"

Such words may be shocking to hear, but your child's outburst is also a sign that he trusts you to keep loving him, no matter what he says to you. It shows that he feels safe enough to express his anger and is confident you won't reject him.

When you love your child so much, it can be upsetting to hear him say something so mean. While he is learning to express his emotions, it is important for you to maintain clear boundaries and not give in to what he wants, despite the intensity of the moment.

WHEN A CHILD SAYS "I HATE YOU," HE IS TRYING TO PUT STRONG EMOTIONS HE DOES NOT KNOW HOW TO EXPRESS INTO SIMPLE WORDS.

WHAT HE'S THINKING

"I hate grown-ups being able to tell me what to do. It's not fair."

The words "I hate you" spring from the emotionally reactive part of your child's brain, not the logical, thinking part—and thinking them is not the same as feeling them. He does not yet have the fluency or self-control to say, "I really like watching this, and I am angry you won't let me watch as much as I want."

SEE RELATED TOPICS
I wish I had a different family: pp.194–195
You never let me do anything: pp.238–239

HOW TO RESPOND

In the moment...

Stay calm. Your child is most likely to be too upset to hear anything you say. So avoid responding with "Well, I love you" or "You know you love me, really," because that dismisses your child's genuine frustration. If you feel hurt, step away from the situation for a minute or two to stay in control of your feelings.

Name the emotions. Your child is in a heightened emotional state, so name his feelings in short, clear sentences to model nonhurtful emotional expression and show that you understand he's upset. Say: "You're angry that you can't watch another episode."

Explore ways of dealing with feelings. When he feels frustrated or angry, suggest that he takes some deep breaths, distracts himself, or tells you what he wishes could happen. Although it will take time to master this, it is the start of your child learning to manage his emotions.

Keep it in perspective. Stay calm by reminding yourself that his words are not personal and it's being given boundaries that he hates, not you. If you overreact to him saying he hates you, these words will become too powerful, and he'll say them more.

In the long term...

Let the dust settle. Don't punish your child. Afterward, he might feel ashamed, so help him process this by explaining to him the difference between hating you and hating the rules, which mean that, for his own well-being, he can't always have what he wants.

"But Mommy said I could."

At this age, your child will try testing limits by talking to one parent toget around the other. No two parents will agree perfectly on all things, but agreeing on some basic rules will reduce confusion, make your home more peaceful, and give your child a sense of security.

SCENARIO | You come home to find your child on a tablet, despite the fact that you agreed to a rule of "no screens during the week."

SHE SAYS

"But Mommy said I could."

Adults often come to parenthood with differing ideas about how children should be brought up. As a result, disagreements over how to parent—especially, sticking to the rules—can cause tension. Working together, though, will help your child understand what is expected of her and minimize conflict.

SEE RELATED TOPICS
It's not fair!: pp.180–181
Stop fighting!: pp.214–215

YOU MIGHT THINK

"We agreed—no screens during the week. Why do I always have to be the one to enforce the rules?"

WHAT SHE'S THINKING

"I want to do this, and Mommy is easier to persuade."

Agreeing on and setting rules is hard work. If you're the stricter parent, you may feel angry when your partner undermines your efforts by giving in. If you're the more lenient parent, you may resent the hassle of enforcing rules you didn't choose. But your child needs to see you as a united front.

Children sense when they can play one parent off against the other. They test to see what they can get away with, but they also feel anxious when the rules are inconsistent. Your child will feel safer and more cared for if both parents are usually on the same page.

HOW TO RESPOND

In the moment...

(1)

Hold your tongue. Avoid angrily criticizing the other parent in front of your child. This scares children and makes them feel like they should take sides. Try asking, "Can I help?" instead of saying, "You're doing it wrong!"

(2)

Reaffirm parental unity. When your child says, "But Mommy lets me do that," reply calmly "Sometimes we can do things a bit differently, but we've both agreed that you need to finish looking at the tablet now."

In the long term...

Work out disagreements privately. Talk about what matters to both of you. Try to find a middle ground, or lean toward the partner who feels more strongly about an issue.

Don't "compensate." Being extra strict won't make up for a too lenient parent, just as being extra lenient won't make up for a too strict parent. Trying to compensate undermines the authority of both parents and teaches kids that they don't have to listen to anyone.

Tolerate minor differences. You and your partner don't have to be in lockstep. Children can handle parents doing some things differently when there's no tension about it.

Good manners

A baby's burps and yawns seem adorable. But not long after toddlers start to walk and talk, they need to start learning how to behave in social settings.

Good manners are more than just saying "please" and "thank you" and using a knife and fork properly; they are also about developing an awareness of the needs and feelings of others—and treating them with respect.

Research has found that good manners are important for making friends and enjoying school and professional success throughout life.

From the age of 2, children can begin to learn good manners, to treat others with kindness and courtesy, and to ask politely for what they want. But fully mastering manners takes a long time. Make sure, though, that your expectations about your child's behavior are in line with what he is capable of developmentally. Consistency, repetition, and patience will be key.

1
Be a good example.
Consistently demonstrate good manners yourself, both in and out of the home. Let your child see you treating family members, friends, acquaintances, and strangers with respect.

4
Have family meals.
The best place to teach manners is at family mealtimes, where eventually, like grown-ups, children will sit at the table, use their cutlery, use their indoor voice, not make noises when they eat, chew with their mouth closed, thank the cook, and wait until the end of the meal to leave the table.

6
Show the results.
Soon children will see how saying "magic" words such as "please" and "thank you" make it more likely they'll have their requests met.

GOOD PRACTICE

8 key principles

2
Start simply.
Prompting your child to say "please" and "thank you" is the easiest way to start teaching manners. Be careful not to overwhelm him with too many rules. Let him master one or two of them before moving on to more.

3
Encourage eye contact.
Looking people in the eye shows friendly interest. To help your child practice, make it a game: ask him to find out the color of the eyes of the people he speaks to.

5
Let him tell you.
See if your school-age child can explain why manners are important. How does he feel when someone is rude to him? What would the world be like if no one used good manners?

7
Compliment them.
Let them overhear you praise their good manners to others and enjoy the positive attention they get when you point out their courteous behavior.

8
Explain that good manners = friendship skills.
Greeting people, smiling, and waiting for their turn to talk are important for getting along with others and making friends.

TAILORED ADVICE

Age by age

2–3
YEARS OLD
Daily greetings
Say "Good morning" to your child every day, and greet other family members, too.

Toy helpers
Use stuffed animals, dolls, or puppets to play mealtimes and practice saying "please," "thank you," "you're welcome," and "excuse me."

4–5
YEARS OLD
A personal note
When children are starting to learn to write and draw, get them to draw or sign their name on thank-you notes, and tell them how happy this makes others feel.

Board game lessons
Playing board games gives children the chance to learn cooperation and turn-taking while having fun.

6–7
YEARS OLD
The host with the most
Before a playdate, talk about greeting guests at the door, asking what they'd like to do, sharing toys, and saying goodbye and "Thanks for visiting!" afterward.

Manners and feelings
Point out how holding a door or giving up a seat for older people makes them feel respected and happy.

"No one likes me."

Having good friends is becoming increasingly important to children at this age. They have now gone beyond playmates to wanting to form stronger bonds with others who share their interests. But if a child gets left out, she will feel hurt.

SCENARIO | **Your child has come out of school and told you she has no friends.**

SHE SAYS

"No one likes me."

YOU MIGHT THINK

"I hate that she feels sad and lonely! But I can't make friends for her."

It's not unusual for kids to say they have no friends from time to time. At this age, children are black-and-white thinkers, so a refusal to play one day may be taken as general dislike. Some need help interpreting social cues from others to know how to join in, take turns, and be a fun playmate.

It's heartbreaking to think of your child alone in a playground, unable to find a friend to play with. Offer comfort first. Save tips about where she may have gone wrong for when she's feeling less raw. Also keep in mind that children's feelings and relationships can change quickly.

EVERY CHILD WILL FEEL FRIENDLESS AT SOME POINT. YOUR ROLE IS TO OFFER PERSPECTIVE AND HELP YOUR CHILD FEEL LOVED AT HOME.

SEE RELATED TOPICS

They're being mean to me: pp.192–193
I'm not playing anymore: pp.224–225

WHAT SHE'S THINKING

"I had no one to play with today. Will anyone like me again?"

Your child is discovering that friendships have ups and downs—but just because she felt lonely today doesn't mean there won't be playmates tomorrow. If she feels rejected at school, it's even more vital that she feels accepted at home.

HOW TO RESPOND

In the moment...

Listen and give her a cuddle. Acknowledge her feelings, and let her know she is loved. Reassure her that friendships change fast and it's always possible to build new friendship skills.

In the long term...

Practice friend-making skills. Children can learn "social smarts," which improve with practice. Help her learn by playing board games (taking turns) and teach her how to connect with others (look people in the eye and smile).

Talk about resolution skills. If your child is having a lot of arguments with her friends, offer some strategies to get through her "friendship rough spots." Help her to learn how to compromise, give in graciously, ask for what she wants, and both accept and give an apology.

Help her learn empathy. If she can learn to better understand how others feel, she can learn to respond with the right words and gestures and will be accepted more. Give her practice by playing a game of watching other children's faces in the playground or on TV and trying to guess their feelings.

Encourage a wide friendship circle. Having more friends as well as friends outside of school will give your child more options for weathering the inevitable ups and downs of friendships.

"They're being mean to me."

It's upsetting when your child tells you that others have been mean to him. It's also natural to want to protect your child from hurt. But as children learn to socialize, they need to learn to cope with a degree of "normal" social pain.

SCENARIO | **Your child tells you that other boys wouldn't let him join in their game at break time.**

HE SAYS

"They're being mean to me."

YOU MIGHT THINK

"Is my child being bullied? Do I need to do something?"

Kids can be mean. They're impulsive and their empathy isn't fully developed, so it's likely that at some point your child will be teased or excluded. Your child might also misinterpret neutral or thoughtless actions as deliberate meanness.

Not every unkind act counts as bullying. Bullying involves deliberate meanness, usually over a period of time and often by a child who is bigger, tougher, or more socially powerful than the one being targeted. Kids can learn to handle ordinary meanness, but bullying requires adult intervention.

◆ SEE RELATED TOPICS ▶
I don't want to go to school: pp.196–197
But all my friends have one: pp.208–209

" "

AS A PARENT, YOUR JOB IS TO TEACH HIM TO DEAL WITH FRIENDSHIP ISSUES HIMSELF.

WHAT HE'S THINKING

"I'm angry and hurt and a little bit scared. I wish a grown-up would make them be nice to me!"

Learning to handle conflict and ordinary meanness is an essential social skill. Offer comfort and ask what happened, step by step, to discover the details, so you can correct misunderstandings or help your child cope.

HOW TO RESPOND

In the moment...

①

Explain that it can change tomorrow. Most conflicts between children are resolved by a brief separation and then just being nice to each other. Tell him that a conflict doesn't have to mean the end of a friendship, and encourage him to try to have fun with the friend tomorrow.

②

Model calmness. Kids who have big emotional reactions to teasing are likely to be teased more. Role-play to teach your child bored responses to teasing, such as "So what?" or "That's so funny I forgot to laugh."

③

Help him see his part. It's easy to notice what someone else does wrong, but your child may have trouble seeing his contribution to conflicts. Gently help your child figure out if he can do something to make things better, such as listening when someone says stop or not being bossy.

In the long term...

Encourage kind friends. If conflicts are frequent, your child may do better hanging out with kids who he feels good being around. Sometimes children stick with mean friends because they think they don't have other options. Joining new activities and having playdates can fuel more promising friendships.

Step in if there's real bullying. If the meanness is ongoing and involves a power difference, you may need to contact the school to help keep your child safe.

"I wish I had a different family."

As a parent, you've done your best to establish a loving home, so when your child is angry with you, it's upsetting to hear her say she wishes she had a different family. Identifying the feelings underneath can help you respond calmly.

SCENARIO | **You tell your child she can't go to a classmate's party because there's a family occasion you all have to attend.**

SHE SAYS

"I wish I had a different family."

YOU MIGHT THINK

"How could she say such a hurtful and ungrateful thing?"

As your child spends more time outside the home, she realizes other families have different rules so will compare yours with theirs. She now also understands that your feelings can be hurt. Since she has lost her temper, she is prepared to say something shocking, in the moment, to express how upset she is.

You may be upset because your child's remark feels like a rejection of the home you've created, your values, and your family unit. Her comment might also bring up guilt or defensiveness about past parenting mistakes, or your present situation, if it's not as happy as you'd like.

SEE RELATED TOPICS

But Mommy said I could: pp.186–187
You never let me do anything: pp.238–239

WHAT SHE'S THINKING

"I really want to go to the party. A different family would let me."

Your child fantasizes that if she were in a different family, with perfect parents, she would be able to go to the party. But she's not really trying to replace you. She's frustrated because she thinks that you don't understand how much she wants to go.

HOW TO RESPOND

In the moment...

Don't take it personally. This is mostly about her tangled feelings of loving you and needing you but also feeling blocked by you from doing what she wants. As the person who loves her unconditionally, you are the safest target for her frustration.

Acknowledge what's underneath. Say, "You're mad that our family event conflicts with the party" or "You're feeling left out because your friends can go and you can't." You'll model kinder ways to express feelings, and she'll feel better, knowing you understand.

Talk through your reasons. When she's calmer, explain why attending the family event is important. She is a key part of the family, and she would be missed.

In the long term...

See her perspective. As children get older, their friends become more important to them. If she has to miss the party, perhaps you can plan another get-together with her friends.

Make family time fun. The best way to keep your child connected to her family is to do fun things together. Consider her interests. You could also allow her to invite a friend along for some family outings.

"I don't want to go to school."

All children have the odd day when they don't feel like going to school. But, apart from illness, there can be other reasons they want to stay at home. If it happens repeatedly over a few weeks, figure out what's worrying your child and why he doesn't want to go.

SCENARIO | Your child refuses to get dressed in the morning and go to school.

HE SAYS

"I don't want to go to school."

YOU MIGHT THINK

"This is frustrating! I know he's not sick, so he has to go to school."

If your child has no symptoms of illness, look for other reasons behind his refusal. Is he tired? Is he struggling with schoolwork or friendship issues? Did he get in trouble at school? Is he worried about leaving you or jealous of a younger sibling who gets to stay home?

Keep the criteria for going to school objective. If he doesn't have a fever, isn't vomiting, or has no obvious symptom, he needs to go. If you let him stay home because he's anxious, you're telling him that going to school is dangerous and making it harder for him to go the next day.

SEE RELATED TOPICS

No one likes me: pp.190–191
Do you have to go to work?: pp.236–237

BE POSITIVE ABOUT SCHOOL AND CALMLY INSIST THAT IT'S HIS JOB TO ATTEND.

WHAT HE'S THINKING

"Home feels safe and calm to me."

Children's bodies are sensitive to emotions. If your child is feeling anxious about something, he'll want the security of being at home with a parent. In fact, he could be so worried that he works himself into having a real tummyache—that magically disappears if he stays home.

HOW TO RESPOND

In the moment...

Hold the line. Be patient with him, and reflect back his emotions so he knows you are listening, but at the same time, be firm and don't cave in. Offer to talk more about his concerns after school.

②

Take your time. If you are becoming stressed, call ahead to school and explain that your child may be in late; and, if necessary, let your employer know so you can stay calm and address the situation thoroughly.

In the long term...

Make mornings manageable. Rushing can make kids feel anxious. Lay out clothes the night before. Make sure your child goes to bed early enough to be rested and wakes early enough to have a calm morning routine.

Help him express himself. Ask your child to create a silly character who says the things that make him anxious. The next time your child hears these worries, ask if his "worry gremlin" is talking loudly or ask what it's saying. This way you can work with him to "fight back" against those thoughts.

Speak to your child's teacher and pediatrician. If there's a pattern emerging, work with the school to identify the problem. It's worth taking your child to the doctor to rule out any physical issues if he often mentions tummyaches and headaches.

"She's my best friend."

When children first go to preschool, they are usually happy to play alongside whoever is nearby. However, by 6 or 7, your child may be seeking out one special "best" friend who she clicks with and whose company she prefers over others.

SCENARIO | Your child has told you that she now has a "best friend."

SHE SAYS

"She's my best friend."

YOU MIGHT THINK

"I'm glad she's found a special buddy, but what if they break up?"

Having a special friend to pair up with at school can make your child feel safer. Because she fears being left out, she will be happy to always have the security of someone who'll want to be her partner. She will also feel proud that someone likes her enough to appoint her as her best friend.

Having a best friend is exciting and fun. However, about half of first graders' friendships don't last a full school year. Most kids who break up with a best friend will find a new one, but don't worry if your child doesn't have a best friend. Children can have fun with a variety of more casual friends, too.

GOOD FRIENDSHIPS WILL HELP YOUR CHILD FEEL HAPPIER AT SCHOOL, BUT NOT EVERY CHILD HAS TO HAVE A BEST FRIEND.

WHAT SHE'S THINKING

"I want to be with my best friend all the time."

The flip side of best friendship is that it can come with strings attached. Children at this age care deeply about having friends, but they think more about what their friends do for them than what they contribute to a friendship. They may also change best friends daily.

HOW TO RESPOND

In the moment...

Support your child's friendship. If your child tells you that she has a best friend, welcome the news and let her introduce the friend, and then arrange time for them to spend together.

Remind her of other friends. Take the opportunity to talk about her other friends and plan playdates with them. And prompt her on including others in games so that this best friendship does not become exclusive and so she does not feel alone when it inevitably hits a sticky patch.

In the long term...

Get her to use other terms as well. Children can also describe others they are in a trusting relationship with as "good" or "close" friends. Explain that if she gives one the title "best friend," she will give the impression that others are less important to her.

Don't see it as the ideal. Best friends can offer security in always having a partner, but not being tied to one person can also offer freedom. As long as your child is happy, it's fine if she has a best friend—and fine if she doesn't. Help her to comprehend this, too.

Be prepared for ups and downs. Research has found that if your child has a best friend, then that person is the one she will have the most arguments with. So be ready to support her through such situations. That said, because of their close relationship, they will also be more invested in making up afterward.

SEE RELATED TOPICS
They're being mean to me: pp.192–193
I've got a boyfriend: pp.222–223

School pressure

Even in elementary school, teachers start preparing children to take standardized tests in certain subjects. Some children may find this work more stressful and difficult than others.

It's common for parents to fret about how their child performs at school. Yet it's important for you to keep this in perspective and remember that schools measure only a limited range of your child's abilities.

Wherever your child sits in the spectrum of academic performance, help him feel competent in lots of other areas of life, especially those that can't be measured in a classroom—qualities such as kindness, generosity, or creativity.

Even if you have a child who scores well on school tests, emphasize that trying, doing his best, learning, and improving are more important than having top grades.

Make it clear that your love for your child is unconditional—he never has to "earn" it with good grades.

1
Value every quality.
Encourage children to see themselves as well-rounded characters who are more than the sum of their achievements on paper. Recognize and praise qualities such as humor, gratitude, kindness, self-control, optimism, and persistence.

4
Celebrate uniqueness.
Rather than compare your child to others, delight in the combination of qualities that makes him uniquely who he is.

6
Praise process.
Instead of praising your child for a fixed skill, such as being "good at math," praise him for the qualities he has control over, such as strategy and effort. Explain that he can always get better at a subject.

SOCIAL AND EMOTIONAL WELL-BEING ARE THE BEST PREDICTORS OF FUTURE HAPPINESS AND SUCCESS, NOT TEST SCORES.

GOOD PRACTICE

8 key principles

2
Use the word "yet."
If children can't do something easily, it's usually because they haven't had the chance to learn or practice how to do it. Emphasize that learning is ongoing and that they will get better at any task with practice and feedback.

3
Create a haven at home.
Aim to make your home a place where your children can retreat from the world and recharge from the school day. Just as important as schoolwork is downtime, fresh air, exercise, and family activities.

5
Compete for their personal best.
Explain that there is just one person who is truly worth beating—themselves. This way, children can always feel a sense of achievement when they improve.

7
Make time for play.
Play and learning are not two different things. Studies show that science and math are best learned through real-life experience. Children will understand money, for example, if they are taught to use it, and science if they spend time outdoors so they can see how key concepts work in the natural world.

8
Explain how his brain works.
Help your child understand that the brain is like a muscle that keeps getting stronger through exercise. Older children may comprehend that neural pathways are built by practice and repetition. The more nerve cells are linked by firing together, the stronger the network becomes, forming a memory and eventually a skill.

TAILORED ADVICE

Age by age

2–3
YEARS OLD

Free play
Even very young children spot when adults try to take control of their games and "teach" them something, so don't turn play into a lesson.

Simple is best
Don't fall for claims on high-tech toys or apps implying they can make your child smarter. Children learn best from the simplest toys.

4–5
YEARS OLD

Competitive parenting
Avoid competing with other parents over reading and math levels. Turning these skills into a race isn't helpful and can be stressful.

Natural talents
Help your child build on the activities he's naturally drawn to, so he feels competent and continues learning.

6–7
YEARS OLD

Actively interested
Ask your child about what he's learning, not what grade he got. Let him teach you, so he can see your eagerness to learn.

Hold back
If your child struggles with academics, offer explanations and support good study habits, but don't correct his work. Teachers need to see what he does or doesn't understand.

"Homework is boring."

Many children get set a certain amount of homework as soon as they start elementary school. But when a child comes home after a day of lessons, often the last thing she wants to do is sit down and do more schoolwork. So many children will make excuses to avoid it.

SCENARIO | **Your child refuses to sit down to complete her math worksheet.**

SHE SAYS

"Homework is boring."

YOU MIGHT THINK

"If she just sat and did her homework, it wouldn't take long."

Clarify what your child means when she says homework is boring. Does she mean that it's not as fun as playing or that she's not sure how to do it? Once you've listened, understood, and helped her look at the task, she's more likely to get down to it.

Your child is learning the skills and self-discipline she needs to do homework. Don't get angry with her repeated refusals. It's tempting to help her do it, but that would send the wrong message—that if she makes enough fuss, you'll do it. Your role is to give her good habits and show her how to take responsibility.

SETTING UP ROUTINES CAN MINIMIZE ARGUMENTS ABOUT WHERE AND WHEN HOMEWORK SHOULD BE DONE.

WHAT SHE'S THINKING

"I don't want to do this homework."

At this developmental stage, sitting and listening in school all day takes a lot of self-control. An after-school snack will help your child refuel. Some kids do best getting homework out of the way early; others need a play before starting homework.

◆ SEE RELATED TOPICS ◆
I'm the worst: pp.210–211
Do I have to do music practice?: pp.230–231

HOW TO RESPOND

In the moment...

①

Don't stress. At your child's age, practicing a bit of math or reading at home can help her gain academic skills and confidence, but learning through play is still essential. If homework becomes dreaded, painful, or lengthy, talk to your child's teacher about how to modify it. Fewer or easier problems, fewer days, or mental rather than written practice are options.

②

Stay positive and close. Model a positive attitude toward schoolwork. If you see it as a dreaded chore, so will your child. Sitting nearby—working cheerfully on your own "homework"—may make it easier for your child to start or continue her work. You're also available if she has questions.

In the long term...

Use "when...then..." Tell your child, "When you do your homework without complaining, then we have time to play a short game together."

Set up a homework base. Create a place to do all homework. The kitchen table is probably the best place so you can be close. Clear away any distractions, such as devices and toys, and equip it with all she needs— pencils, erasers, and crayons.

Make it fun. Being playful can make homework more fun. Set up an audience of admiring stuffed animals to watch your child do work. Use a puppet who gets excited when she gets a problem right. Dance or move to make math facts active. Talk with a silly accent. Read books on topics she finds fascinating.

"I'm the best."

As the approval of peers becomes more important, children sometimes think that others will like them more if they say they are particularly good at something. However, they may not yet realize that bragging can be annoying.

SCENARIO | **Your child keeps telling other kids that he is the best goal scorer in soccer.**

HE SAYS

"I'm the best."

Children are now becoming aware of how they are different and will start to compare their achievements, skills, and possessions with others. Your child may believe that if other children are impressed by him, they will want to be his friend.

HELP CHILDREN KNOW THAT FRIENDSHIP INVOLVES CONNECTING RATHER THAN IMPRESSING.

SEE RELATED TOPICS
They're being mean to me: pp.192–193
I'm not as good as them: pp.220–221

YOU MIGHT THINK

"Other children won't like him if he keeps bragging or showing off."

It's good that your child takes pride and has confidence in his abilities. As any proud parent, you want to give him due praise, but you may be tempted to ask him to pipe down about his skills, since no one likes a show-off. Talk about how giving compliments to others makes them feel good, too.

WHAT HE'S THINKING

"I like the idea of being better than everyone."

Your child may not understand that bragging does not draw others to him. He does not yet realize that celebrating his successes can make others feel as if they are falling short. He may need help in understanding how friends feel when he keeps reminding them he is the best.

HOW TO RESPOND

In the moment...

Talk about feelings. Acknowledge that it feels good to do something well, but saying, "I'm better than you!" is unkind. Your child can enjoy his growing skills without putting others down.

Discuss friendship. Tell him that friendship is about enjoying other people's company, not proving to them how amazing you are. To connect with other children, show him how to look for what he has in common with others, not what sets him apart.

In the long term...

See more than achievement. To make sure your child knows that love doesn't have to be earned, express delight in other qualities, such as his sweet smile or how he keeps you company when you go grocery shopping.

Avoid overblown praise. It may be tempting to tell kids they're amazingly good or "the best" to try to boost their self-esteem, but research has found that inflated praise promotes narcissism. Comments, such as "You did it!" or "Nice pass!" are more accurate and encouraging.

Focus on progress. Instead of comparing to others, encourage your child to compare his current and past abilities to develop healthy pride. You could say, "Last year, you were afraid to put your face in the water, but now you can swim!"

"You're embarrassing me."

In the early years, your child probably told you that you were the kindest and bravest Mommy in the world or the funniest and most generous Daddy. So it can come as a shock the first time your child says you act in a way that is embarrassing to her.

SCENARIO | **Your child has said she does not want you to kiss her goodbye on the school playground anymore.**

SHE SAYS

"You're embarrassing me."

YOU MIGHT THINK

"I'm sad that she no longer wants me to kiss her in public."

As social awareness increases around this age, your child notices what other children and families do and how they differ from her family. She might also hear other children talking about these differences and not want to stick out.

You are likely to feel hurt that the golden period when your child thought you could do no wrong has come to an end. But she still loves and needs you. She's just learning about social norms, which is a sign that her brain is growing. Try not to see this as a personal rejection.

SEE RELATED TOPICS

No one likes me: pp.190–191
You never let me do anything: pp.238–239

WHAT SHE'S THINKING

"My friends don't get goodbye kisses. I don't want them either."

As your child becomes more independent, she won't want to do things in public that she considers babyish. She'll probably still want your kisses at home, but she's anxious about other children teasing her for being different.

HOW TO RESPOND

In the moment...

Don't get angry. Your child doesn't mean to be hurtful. This is about her more than you. She's trying to figure out what's "normal" among her peers and doesn't want to be treated like a baby.

②

Respect the requests—within reason. Now that your child is becoming more self-conscious, adapt to reasonable requests—treating her in a more grown-up way in front of others. These are a necessary part of development and a sign that she's becoming her own person.

In the long term...

Negotiate the guidelines. To be sensitive to your child, you could ask her when she's happy for you to give her kisses and cuddles outside the home and when she'd rather you held back.

Insist on kindness. Your child can ask for what she wants without putting you down. Use "I feel" statements to explain how you felt when she told you that you were embarrassing and talk about what she could have said instead.

Discuss fitting in. Talk with your child about what makes your family different and how she feels about that. Some things you might be willing to adjust; but others, such as observing the Sabbath, learning your family's native culture or language, or being vegetarian, are central to who you are, so you'll proudly hold on to these differences.

FINDING PUBLIC PARENTAL AFFECTION EMBARRASSING IS A SIGN THAT KIDS WANT TO MOVE BEYOND BEING BABIED.

"But all my friends have one."

As children become more aware of their place among peers, they learn that fitting in makes them feel happy. And to fit in, they may say that they "need" new devices, toys, or clothes. How you respond is a chance to put possessions into perspective.

SCENARIO | **Your child has asked for his own tablet so he can play the latest video games.**

HE SAYS

"But all my friends have one."

YOU MIGHT THINK

"I don't want him to feel left out, but that tablet is expensive."

Your child is now exposed to more media and programs with advertisements, many of which are aimed directly at him to encourage pestering. As he starts to compare himself to others, he is affected by a powerful new force—fear of missing out. He wants what he thinks his friends have to feel "normal."

It's fun to buy things for your child that he enjoys. You may also feel some pressure to buy an item so your child isn't the odd one out. On the other hand, budget and values could influence your purchase decisions.

SEE RELATED TOPICS
No one likes me: pp.190–191
I'm not as good as them: pp.220–221

HOW TO RESPOND

In the moment...

Ask why he wants it. Get a sense of why it appeals to him. Acknowledge his wish, but also talk about the difference between "needs" and "wants."

Put his request into perspective. Do all his friends really have one, as he claims? By talking to other parents, you may find out that's not actually the case.

③

Facilitate his wants within limits. If you simply give your child the tablet right away, he may take it for granted that he will always get what he wants. Instead, ask if he would like to put his request on a "waiting list" to see if he wants it as much in a few weeks' time or suggest he hangs on until his birthday or Christmas.

Help him value the personal. Explain that cool toys won't necessarily help him make friends. The real reason other children want to spend time with him is because he's fun to be with, cooperates, and is fair in games.

In the long term...

Stand up to peer pressure. If your child talks about what his friends' parents allow, use the phrase "in our family" to help him understand that different families have different values and priorities.

WHAT HE'S THINKING

"I really, really need it. My friends have it, so I should have one, too."

Your child might want the device because it's fun, he wants to be "cool," he wants to be included in peer activities, or he wants to be just like his friends. He doesn't yet realize that he can want without having and that his personal qualities matter more that what he owns.

"I'm the worst."

At this age, parents want children to start to take responsibility for their actions. But when they make mistakes, some children may wrongly see them as evidence that they are totally bad. Their guilt and shame are completely out of proportion to their "crime."

SCENARIO | **Your child knocks your favorite mug off the table and breaks it.**

SHE SAYS

"I'm the worst."

Your child wants to be good, but her thinking is black and white, so when she disappoints you or does something wrong, she feels totally bad. Rather than see this accident as an understandable mistake, she is using catastrophic thinking to tell herself she never does anything right.

SEE RELATED TOPICS
I can't do it: pp.182–183
My legs are too fat: pp.242–243

YOU MIGHT THINK

"I'm mad that she broke it, but she's overreacting!"

If the mug was precious, you're understandably angry at your child's carelessness. You may even have lashed out, in the heat of the moment, with some less-than-kind remarks. But you certainly don't want her to feel worthless. You may feel alarmed by her harsh self-blame.

MAKING MISTAKES IS A NORMAL PART OF GROWING UP. HELP YOUR CHILD TO LEARN FROM THEM IN A CONSTRUCTIVE, SHAME-FREE WAY.

WHAT SHE'S THINKING

"I'm an idiot. Why do I always do stupid things?"

Your child is magnifying this one mistake into a verdict on her worth as a human being. This event also brings up memories of other mistakes she's made, compounding her shame. She may believe she's supposed to beat herself up when she does something wrong.

HOW TO RESPOND

In the moment...

Say **"it's okay" and mean it.** Explain that mistakes are a part of life and that people are more important than things. Tell her you know she's sorry and you forgive her.

Tell her to be kind to herself. The opposite of shame is compassion. Point out that she wouldn't say those mean things to a friend, so she shouldn't say them to herself.

Help her make amends. This allows her to let go of her guilt. She could fix or replace the mug, do an extra chore, or make a plan for how she can be more careful.

In the long term...

Be gentle with criticism. In some cases, children put themselves down to prevent their parents from criticizing them. If you suspect that's the case, you may need to tone down the frequency or intensity with which you correct your sensitive child.

Model anti-perfectionism. Perfectionism is a trap that makes people feel like nothing they do is ever good enough. When you make a mistake, let your child hear you say aloud, "Oh, well. Everyone makes mistakes" or "It's not perfect, but it's good enough."

Money matters

To a child, money is a commodity that allows grown-ups to go into stores and take whatever they want. It takes many stages of development to understand what money is, but there's plenty you can do to guide your child.

Although many parents may think children don't yet need to know about the economic realities of life, research has found that it's better to get children into good money habits when they are young—in fact, attitudes toward saving and spending are set by the age of 7.

Giving pocket money also plays an important part in teaching children mental arithmetic. What's more: having to deal with regular amounts of money is one of the best ways to train children how to control their impulses, learn patience, have willpower, and delay gratification. When children find that saving up their pocket money for something they really want feels better than simply spending it all at once on frivolous stuff, it's a milestone in their self-regulation. Plus, practicing how to save now will set them up with sensible money habits for life.

"

SHOPPING WITH YOUR CHILD AND TALKING THROUGH SPENDING DECISIONS IS TRAINING FOR THE FUTURE.

1
Let them practice with cash.
Let your child participate in small purchases by checking the price, paying the cashier, receiving change, and taking the item home.

4
Teach them where money comes from.
Unless told otherwise, young children think money is free and that banks and ATMs give it out to anyone. Help them understand that money is earned by going to work.

6
Explain finite finances.
Young children find it hard to grasp that money can be spent only once. Give them $1 to go shopping to see that once it's gone, it's gone.

9
Don't tie allowance to chores.
Don't make your child earn pocket money. Chores are jobs your child does to pitch in, for the good of the family, not because he's paid.

!

GOOD PRACTICE

12 key principles

2

Show purchase options.
Help your child understand different values and see the trade-off between buying something small now and saving up to buy something better later.

3

Get them into saving and giving.
Put pocket money into three jars: one for spending, one for saving for bigger-ticket items, and one for giving to the charity of your child's choice.

5

Show its limits.
Talk through your own shopping choices, showing how you make decisions about what is and isn't good value. Such chats will make it clear that you can't afford everything you want.

7

Explain card spending.
In an increasingly cashless world, explain that when you use a card, it's the same as having money taken out of your bank account.

8

Let them make mistakes.
Even if you disagree with his spending decisions, allow your child to make mistakes. It's better to learn with small amounts at a young age than bigger amounts later on.

10

Let them earn extra.
Come up with some other jobs that your child can do to earn extra money. This allows him to see a link between effort and income.

11

Be consistent.
Give children pocket money at the same time each week in the same way as a salary so they can start to manage their money.

12

Don't give it upfront.
Try not to pay out in advance. If they ask, charge a small amount of interest so they realize that it costs money to borrow money.

TAILORED ADVICE

Age by age

2–3
YEARS OLD

Play with money
Show children how money can be exchanged for goods by playing store and coffee shop with them.

Show that size matters
Children at this age believe that one coin can buy anything. Point out how different coins and dollars can buy items of different value.

4–5
YEARS OLD

Explain earnings
Children believe that everyone has money, given to them for free by banks or shopkeepers. Explain how money is earned.

Teach generosity
At this age, children can start to imagine others' thoughts and feelings. Introduce the idea of charitable giving through volunteering and family donations.

6–7
YEARS OLD

Give them some cash
Now that children can count and understand how money works, it's time for you to start regular pocket money.

Encourage savings
Teach them that saving is a good thing, and praise them for their self-control when they save up their cash. Help them see the amount grow in a glass jar.

"Stop fighting!"

Most parents will argue in front of their children at some point. It can be difficult to think clearly when emotions are running high, but how you handle these conflicts is crucial for your child's well-being and her understanding of how relationships work.

SCENARIO | **During an argument with your partner, your child shouts at you both to stop fighting.**

SHE SAYS

"Stop fighting!"

YOU MIGHT THINK

"I'm so angry. I didn't notice she was listening."

Your child may not understand the reasons, but she still registers the conflict. Studies show that even young babies show a rise in blood pressure and stress hormones when they hear their parents shouting in anger. She depends on you for everything, so to her, this feels like an earthquake.

You may feel guilty because you know that it's upsetting for your child to see you arguing, but when you're furious at your partner, it can be hard to rein yourself in. The reactive, fight-or-flight part of your brain takes over and overcomes your rational thinking.

VIEW YOU AND YOUR PARTNER AS BEING ON THE SAME TEAM AND AN ARGUMENT AS A PROBLEM TO BE SOLVED, NOT A CONTEST TO WIN.

WHAT SHE'S THINKING

"What will happen to me if they break up?"

Your child believes that adults in relationships should be loving all the time, so if she hears you say cruel things to each other, she may think you're splitting up. Because it's scarier to think they have no control, children tend to believe it's their fault you're fighting and their job to stop it.

▶ SEE RELATED TOPICS ▶
But Mommy said I could: pp.186–187
I wish I had a different family: pp.194–195

HOW TO RESPOND

In the moment...

Calm yourself. There are always two problems in an argument: your emotions running out of control and the actual problem. Protect your child from witnessing the former by recognizing when your reactive "lower brain" has taken over. Show your child that you are calming down and say that you and your partner will talk about it later.

Reassure her. Above all, children want to feel safe, so tell your child an argument doesn't mean you don't love each other. Acknowledge the disagreement, making it clear that it wasn't her fault, even if you were arguing about something connected to her. Say "Daddy and I were angry with each other. Now we're working it out."

Use the conflict to teach your child about emotions. If they see you make up and move on, children can learn that even happy couples disagree, anger is a normal emotion, there's nothing wrong with expressing it, and communicating well can resolve disputes.

In the long term...

Don't drive it underground. You may think it's better not to show open conflict, but using passive-aggressive tactics, such as the silent treatment, is more confusing to children who still pick up on the tension.

Look for ways to sort out your differences. If a child keeps witnessing unresolved fights, it can trigger anxiety, sleep disturbances, concentration problems, and difficulties with peers. After a fight, write down everything that caused it, without blame or accusation, so you can talk it through with your partner calmly.

"But I'm not tired."

Even though getting enough sleep is essential for their growth, health, and learning, children spend a lot of effort fighting going to bed. These battles can be stressful for the whole family and increase your child's resistance to bedtime.

SCENARIO | **It's time for bed, but your child keeps dawdling and delaying, resisting your efforts to call it a night.**

SLEEP IS JUST AS IMPORTANT AS HEALTHY EATING AND EXERCISE FOR DEVELOPMENT.

HE SAYS
—
"But I'm not tired."

Overtired children sometimes get a second wind. As you're trying to help him settle down for the night, he might be running around, teasing his brother, or suddenly fascinated by all the things he could play with. He's not mature enough to understand the idea of "Sleep now, or you'll be tired later." Going to bed seems boring.

SEE RELATED TOPICS

It's not fair!: pp.180–181
You never let me do anything: pp.238–239

YOU MIGHT THINK

"If he doesn't get enough sleep, he'll be tired and grumpy when he wakes up tomorrow."

WHAT HE'S THINKING

"I don't want to go to sleep. I want to stay up and keep playing."

At the end of the day, you're exhausted. You know your child needs sleep, and you probably have things you need to get done after he's in bed. So it's aggravating when he resists bedtime. You may also dread dealing with a grumpy child tomorrow.

Staying up late seems exciting and grown-up to your child. He doesn't want to miss anything, especially if an older sibling is staying up. It's hard for him to shift from playing to lying quietly in the dark by himself.

HOW TO RESPOND

In the moment...

Create a peaceful routine. Doing the same thing every night helps him associate the routine with sleepiness. Include a cozy activity you'll both enjoy and look forward to, such as a chat, back rub, song, or story time.

Address anxiety. Sometimes fears cause children to resist bedtime. Try talking about worries earlier in the day, using a dim night-light, teaching him to visualize happy scenes, or agreeing to peek at him every 5 minutes if he lies quietly in his bed.

In the long term...

Introduce a digital sunset. Make sure your child turns off electronic gadgets at least an hour before bedtime. Blue light and fast-moving graphics also rev up his brain, making it much harder for him to transition to sleep.

Reset his bedtime. As they get older and have more to do after school, children's bedtime can creep later, and their mood, concentration, and schoolwork can suffer. To figure out his bedtime, count back 10½ hours from when he gets up. Then stick to it.

Stay calm and speak softly. If you lose your temper and start yelling, scolding, or barking orders, you'll add to the tension instead of helping him settle. If bedtime often ends with angry voices and tears, it's time to create a new routine that's more pleasant for everyone.

"I'm bored."

Children are usually bursting with enthusiasm, so when your child says she's bored, you might feel worried that you are not stimulating her enough. But children need to be left to their own devices so they learn to direct themselves.

SCENARIO | **Your child says there is nothing to do, and she's not interested in any of her toys or games.**

SHE SAYS

"I'm bored."

YOU MIGHT THINK

"She has so many toys, books, and games. How can she possibly be bored?"

Boredom can be a good thing—it's a sign your child has the free time to do whatever she likes. "I'm bored" can also mean she's lonely and wants to play with a friend, she's worried about something and can't focus, she's feeling low energy and needs to get outside, or she wants your attention.

Many parents fall into the trap of believing they must be constantly "building" their child's brain with all sorts of activities. But research shows that having nothing to do stimulates a child's thinking and boosts creativity.

LEARNING HOW TO BEAT BOREDOM IS A CRUCIAL LIFE SKILL. IT TAKES EFFORT AND PRACTICE TO WORK OUT WHAT TO DO WITH THEMSELVES.

WHAT SHE'S THINKING

"There's no school, no screens, and only myself to play with. What am I supposed to do now?"

Sometimes children complain of boredom if they're looking for something to fully engage their brain or if they're unsure of what to do next. Over time, your child will get better at figuring out what to do without adult guidance and, in doing so, will get to know herself better.

HOW TO RESPOND

In the moment...

Acknowledge her feelings. Just comment, "You're having trouble figuring out what to do" or "Nothing seems appealing right now." Then express confidence in her ability to solve this. Ask, "What do you think might help?" or say, "I'm sure you'll figure out something."

Resist the urge to rescue. If you list a bunch of things she can do, she will reject all your suggestions. No one has ever died of boredom. Just wait and something wonderful will happen—your child will think of something to do!

Pay attention to the physical. Sometimes "I'm bored" means "I'm tired" or "I need exercise." Getting enough sleep and having time outside to run around are important for your child's mood, energy, and well-being.

In the long term...

Embrace the gift of boredom. "Having nothing to do" gives your child a chance to daydream, decompress, explore, and let her imagination run free. Set family guidelines about electronics to make sure she doesn't avoid boredom through excessive use of screens.

Set aside more free play. Research shows that extracurricular activities mean children have far less unstructured time than ever before. This can leave children feeling at a loss when they do have some. Give your child more free time, so she develops hobbies and pastimes to entertain herself.

◄ SEE RELATED TOPICS ►
Homework is boring: pp.202–203
After-school activities: pp.244–245

"I'm not as good as them."

For the parent of a child who has only just started formal lessons at school, it can be worrisome to hear him say he already can't keep up. Your support can help sustain his motivation to continue learning.

SCENARIO | Your child says he is at the table where all of the children who find math hard sit.

HE SAYS

"I'm not as good as them."

YOU MIGHT THINK

"His confidence is so low. I hate hearing him put himself down."

Now that your child is at school, surrounded by a class of other children, he is starting to be able to compare himself to others in a realistic way. His self-appraisal, though painful to hear, is a natural part of his development, and it's now more important than ever to encourage him to embrace learning and believe he can improve.

We all want our children to succeed in school, so it's worrying to hear your child say he thinks he's less capable than his classmates. Empty reassurance won't boost his confidence, but gaining competence will.

SEE RELATED TOPICS
I don't want to go to school: pp.196–197
My legs are too fat: pp.242–243

ENCOURAGE YOUR CHILD TO COMPETE WITH HIMSELF, NOT WITH OTHERS, BECAUSE HE WILL IMPROVE AND ALWAYS WIN.

HOW TO RESPOND

In the moment...

①

Listen first. While it may be tempting to say, "Don't be silly; you're very smart," it's better to acknowledge rather than dismiss his feelings. Say, "You're feeling frustrated right now" or "You're struggling with this lesson."

②

Offer warm encouragement. Express your confidence that your child will be able to learn. Be gentle and patient as you explain concepts or help him practice skills. Tell him children learn at different rates but you know he can master math.

③

Be inspiring. If you tell your child that you weren't good at math, either, this sends the message that he's doomed to find math difficult. Instead, give examples of how you improved by applying yourself.

In the long term...

Celebrate progress. The relationship between effort and success has to be learned. Your child needs to experience many small victories to be willing to keep trying.

Reinforce other talents. Remind your child there are lots of ways of being "smart" that don't relate to school.

WHAT HE'S THINKING

"I'm bad at math, so I'll never be able to learn this."

Children this age are "always" or "never" thinkers. Your child may believe that because he doesn't excel at math at this moment, he'll never master it. This idea can turn into ongoing negative self-talk, which makes it harder for him to think clearly or even try at math.

"I've got a boyfriend."

As they become more aware of the differences between boys and girls, most children prefer to play with friends of the same gender. However, if they have a friend of the other sex, some may copy adults by calling each other "boyfriend" or "girlfriend."

SCENARIO | **Your child comes home with a card from a boy in her class, saying: "To my girlfriend."**

SHE SAYS

"I've got a boyfriend."

YOU MIGHT THINK

"She's too young for a boyfriend. Where is she getting this idea from?"

A boyfriend is most likely a boy who is a friend. But she could mean someone she finds handsome or even innocently loves. They may give each other hugs or pecks on the cheek or talk about getting married when they grow up.

Just as young children play "house," they might also role-play romantic relationships. Your child picks up ideas about boyfriends and girlfriends from movies, TV, books, and real life. Claiming a boyfriend could reflect genuine friendship, a bid for social status, or an attempt to plan her future adult life.

BOY-GIRL FRIENDSHIPS CAN BE AS FUN AND CARING AS SAME-GENDER FRIENDSHIPS.

WHAT SHE'S THINKING

"He's a boy and he's my friend, so isn't he my boyfriend?"

Your child is exploring how the "rules" of society work and may well have overheard grown-ups, siblings, or classmates talking about boyfriends and girlfriends. Most children won't think anything of playing with the other gender until they are made more self-conscious about it by adults or peers.

HOW TO RESPOND

In the moment...

Ask what she means. Find out what your child means by "boyfriend." It may be wishful thinking on her part, or the other child may not realize how he's being described.

Explain the difference. Tell her that a friend who's a boy is not the same as a "boyfriend." Explain that only older people have boyfriend or girlfriend relationships.

Don't elaborate. Resist telling your child how adorable it is to have a boyfriend. Also avoid describing this friendship in adult terms or playing up its importance by teasing her or asking for progress reports.

In the long term...

Get together. If your child and her boyfriend genuinely seem to be friends, organize a playdate. You'll soon see how they play together.

Encourage lots of friendships. Boy-girl friendships occur most often outside of school, between neighbors or family friends. Your child may also feel drawn to the play that's typical of the other gender. These relationships may fade if there's too much teasing from peers, so be sure your child has other friendship options.

SEE RELATED TOPICS
They're being mean to me: pp.192–193
She's my best friend: pp.198–199

"I'm not playing anymore!"

At this age, competitive games are increasingly part of children's play. Learning to handle winning and losing graciously is a difficult but important skill. Being a poor sport can hurt your child's social relationships.

SCENARIO | **Your child says he no longer wants to play a game of cards with a friend because he is losing.**

HE SAYS

"I'm not playing anymore!"

Starting around age 5, children begin playing games with rules and winners and losers. Your child loves the feeling of winning, but tolerating losing is difficult. It's common for kids this age to cheat, try to change the rules, or quit in a huff.

YOUR CHILD MAY NOT REALIZE IT'S SOMETIMES BETTER TO LOSE A GAME THAN A FRIEND.

YOU MIGHT THINK

"If he's a sore loser, no one will want to play with him."

You may feel embarrassed or annoyed by your child's poor sportsmanship, but keep in mind that many children aren't reliably good at taking losing in stride until they're about 9 years old.

SEE RELATED TOPICS

No one likes me: pp.190–191
I'm the best: pp.204–205

WHAT HE'S THINKING

"It feels horrible to lose! I can't bear it."

Your child desperately wants to win because he sees losing as a verdict on his merit. If he loses, he thinks he's a loser. Period. End of story. He can't yet see beyond the moment to understand that winning and losing are temporary.

HOW TO RESPOND

In the moment...

Talk about how to cope with losing. Before the game begins or in a calm moment, teach your child how to respond when the game ends: win or lose, he needs to smile and say, "Good game!" Ask him to tell you why that's important. (So the game is fun for everyone!)

Explain that it's temporary. Ask your child how long winning or losing lasts. The game ends, people say "Good game," "Congratulations!" or "Nice try!" Then they move on. It's over in less than 5 minutes.

Discuss sportsmanship. Ask him to explain why it's important to play fairly. Point out that no one likes to play with cheaters and an unearned victory is meaningless. Talk about professional athletes who are or aren't good sports.

In the long term...

Build his tolerance. Help your child practice handling losing with beat-your-own-record contests, such as marking how far he can jump. Help him work his way up to coping with longer competitive games or team sports.

Explain the goal. Your child can't always win the game, but he can win the fun by having a good time playing.

The digital world

Smartphones, laptops, and tablets are part of daily life, and even very young children are on devices and online. It's crucial that parents help children learn to navigate the digital world safely.

While many children may feel confident about using the Internet, they're not mature enough to fully comprehend all the risks. That's why your guidance and supervision are vital to keeping your child safe online.

At their best, screen-time activities support and supplement real-life interests and relationships. Video calls with far-away relatives can be a great way to stay in touch. Websites and online games can encourage children's creativity, logical thinking, and active learning, but young children still learn best from direct experience with the physical world.

Make sure screen time doesn't overshadow other activities, such as being with friends or playing outside. The digital world can be hypnotizing, so you need to create rules about if, when, and how long your child can use devices.

" "

HELP YOUR CHILD LEARN HOW TO USE THE INTERNET SAFELY AND APPROPRIATELY FOR HER AGE.

1
Limit screen time.
Research shows that it's a good idea to have no more than 1 hour of screen time of high-quality apps or games a day for 2–5-year-olds.

4
Search in safety.
Set up a favorites list of agreed websites and kid-safe search engines so her search results are age appropriate.

6
Do spot checks.
Tell your child that you'll check her browsing history regularly, to keep her safe.

9
Say "no" to a phone.
Phones are powerful minicomputers. While kids may be asking for a phone, it's too early to give them this sort of capacity. Wait until they hit the tween or teen years.

12 *key principles*

2
Set a good example.
Set aside time with your children when you are not using your phone, and be a good role model with your own digital use.

3
Have screen-free times.
Keep mealtimes, coming-home times, and days out tech-free so devices don't interrupt family time. Children will have an easier time with this if the whole family complies.

5
Buy an alarm clock.
Go low-tech with a wake-up alarm, and keep all devices out of your child's bedroom at night. This way your child won't be tempted to be on a device when she should be sleeping.

7
Make tech visible.
Keep devices in common areas, such as the kitchen, so you can see how she's using the Internet and share her discoveries.

8
Stay informed.
Ask about the games, apps, or sites your child enjoys. Let her feel competent by teaching you. Play or visit them with her so you can understand their appeal.

10
Plan for problems.
If your child sees anything upsetting, tell her to turn the device facedown and go tell an adult. Promise she won't get in trouble. You're there to help.

11
Respect age restrictions.
The minimum age for many social media sites is 13. Giving access before then means she may not be ready for the things she's exposed to there.

12
No gadgets at bedtime.
Put devices away an hour before bedtime to prevent blue light from disrupting sleep. Story time with you is a more relaxing end to the day.

Age by age

2–3
YEARS OLD

You decide
Young children are fascinated by digital devices, but your child will not be "behind" if you decide to wait to introduce these.

Keep it active and brief
If you want your child to explore using digital devices, do it together. Play with photos or video and find age-appropriate apps that allow her to take an active role. Keep sessions under half an hour.

4–5
YEARS OLD

Screen-free rewards Tell your child how much you love to play games where you play directly with one another—Snap or Snakes and Ladders—rather than have a screen in the way.

Help with special needs
Devices can help children with disabilities gain independence, inclusion, and improved learning by reducing distractions or increasing sensory input

6–7
YEARS OLD

Privacy is paramount
Explain that she must never share personal information or private photos online.

Beware of marketing
Steer your child away from videos about toys and websites that encourage the purchase of virtual items.

"Where do babies come from?"

At this age, children are starting to hear from their friends about how grown-ups make babies. Be ready to explain sex in a sensitive, age-appropriate way to answer you child's questions and keep the conversation open.

SCENARIO | Your child has heard from his friends about how mommies and daddies make babies. He wants to know if it's true.

HE SAYS

"Where do babies come from?"

YOU MIGHT THINK

"I can't believe he's asking about this already! I'm not sure what to say."

Children are now curious about their place in the world and where they came from. If they don't get the facts, they may use "magical thinking," which means they make up a story to explain what they don't yet understand. For example, they may imagine that when someone wants a baby, all they have to do is go to the hospital and ask for one.

You may feel nervous because you don't know how much to tell, and you don't want to scare or confuse your child. You may also be uncomfortable talking about such an intimate topic, but your child just wants the main facts.

SEE RELATED TOPICS

What's a stranger?: pp.232–233
My diary—keep out!: pp.234–235

WHAT HE'S THINKING

"I've heard kids talk about the daddy putting his penis into the mommy to make a baby, but that can't be true."

Your child is now more aware of the physical differences between boys and girls. What he has heard may sound bizarre or even disgusting to him. He may be asking for reassurance that the truth is not as strange as it sounds. But, at this stage, he can handle only an introduction to the simple mechanics of reproduction.

HOW TO RESPOND

In the moment...

Ask your child what he's heard. Where does he think babies come from? Once you understand his level of knowledge, you will be able to clear up any misunderstandings.

Give the basics. Use straightforward language you are comfortable with. For instance, say, "A special type of seed, called sperm, comes out of a daddy's penis and swims up a mommy's vagina to find her egg. When they meet, a baby can start to grow."

Stop at the right time. If your child reacts with a "yuck," just tell him it's what grown-ups sometimes do to feel close and show love. Stop the conversation if there are no more questions. That means he has enough information and needs time to process it.

In the long term...

Keep talking. As your child gets older, you can add more context, such as how sex is something nice for adults who love each other. If your child hasn't asked by age 9, you may want to start the conversation before peers do.

Use resources. Books specifically written by experts to educate children about sex can guide conversations with your child.

"Do I have to do music practice?"

Music lessons are often seen as one of the best gifts you can give a child. Research suggests that playing a musical instrument benefits coordination as well as social and emotional development. Children like the idea of playing an instrument but aren't so keen on practicing.

SCENARIO | Your child says she hates practicing the piano and complains about having to go to music lessons at all.

SHE SAYS

"Do I have to do music practice?"

For many children, music practice follows a cycle: at the beginning of the week, when their piece is new, and they're not sure they can master it, they resist practice. Later in the week, when the piece feels more familiar and manageable, they're more willing to practice.

YOU MIGHT THINK

"I want her to love music. She has to practice in order to learn."

Music is a pleasure, but learning to play an instrument takes time and effort. Your job is to make the effort doable and even fun, so your child can persist, gain confidence, and experience the joy of playing music.

SEE RELATED TOPICS
It's not fair!: pp.180–181
Homework is boring: pp.202–203

WHAT SHE'S THINKING

"Learning this piece is difficult. I don't know if I can do it."

The relationship between effort and success has to be learned. Your child needs many experiences of overcoming small struggles and gaining mastery to understand and believe that the "I can't do this" stage is temporary.

HOW TO RESPOND

In the moment...

Be an appreciative audience. Tell your child how much you enjoy hearing her play. If she feels criticized, she will become self conscious about practicing or hopeless about improving.

Enjoy it together. Many young children practice best if a parent is nearby, encouraging them or helping if they get stuck. You may even want to make up silly lyrics or dance moves to go along with her pieces. Keep practice sessions brief and fun so she wants to keep with them.

In the long term...

Let your child decide the details. Let her decide when, where (if possible), and how she practices. Having some say will increase her cooperation.

Choose the right teacher. Your child's music teacher should be kind, encouraging, and good at engaging the enthusiasm of young children. At this early stage, delight in making music is the key.

Be flexible. If battles about music practice are intense and ongoing, your child is not developing a love of music. You may need to find a different teacher, choose a different intstrument, or explore an interest that's a better fit for her.

"What's a stranger?"

When your child was a baby and then a toddler, he was always with you or a trusted adult. Now that he's becoming more independent, you may worry about his safety in the wider world. Equipping him with the skills he needs will help keep him safe.

SCENARIO | **During a family trip to the beach, your child mentions that at school he learned about stranger danger.**

HE SAYS

"What's a stranger?"

YOU MIGHT THINK

"I don't want him to worry, but he needs to know how to stay safe."

Because your child has always been surrounded by people he feels are there to look after him, he is likely to believe that all adults are safe. It may be both shocking and confusing to hear you say that some grown-ups might not always have his best interests at heart.

The idea of their child being kidnapped by a stranger strikes terror into the heart of any parent. But children are at much greater risk of being hurt by an adult they know. Your best bet is to help your child learn to recognize and avoid unsafe situations and come to you with concerns.

AS YOUR CHILD BECOMES MORE INDEPENDENT, FIND A MIDDLE GROUND BETWEEN KEEPING HIM SAFE AND ALLOWING HIM TO EXPLORE THE WORLD.

HOW TO RESPOND

In the moment...

Explain simply. Rather than talk about evil "baddies," explain that, while most people are good, some "tricky" adults don't want to keep children safe.

Avoid saying "don't talk to strangers." Suggest instead that he look out for behavior that makes him feel uncomfortable, such as a much older child, teen, or grown-up asking him for help instead of asking an adult. Teach him to watch for "uh-oh" feelings and to listen to those before worrying about being polite, even with other children. Point out helpful strangers so he knows who to go to for help if he gets separated from you. A police officer, employee with a name tag, or mom with young children are good options.

In the long term...

Coach him. When you're out with your child, play "what if" quizzes asking him what he would do in different situations, for example "What if you got lost in a big store?"

Tell him to ask you. Ask your child to always "check first" with you or the person looking after him if someone he doesn't know asks him to do something.

Keep perspective. Don't allow your anxieties to get in the way of letting your child explore the wider world. Being abducted by a stranger is extremely rare. Give greater priority to teaching him other safety skills, such as how to swim, cross the street, and stay safe online.

WHAT HE'S THINKING

"Why would a stranger want to hurt me? How do I know who they are?"

Children this age may be confused about strangers and may not understand that some unsafe people seem friendly and charming. Remind him that he's the boss of his body and should say no and tell you right away if anyone tries to make him do something that makes him scared or uncomfortable.

SEE RELATED TOPICS

Where do babies come from?: pp.228–229
I want a phone: pp.240–241

"My diary—keep out!"

As your child starts to understand her own personal thoughts and feelings better, she may start to write a diary in which she can express things she wants to keep private. While it may be tempting to read her diary, it's best to respect her privacy.

SCENARIO | **You're cleaning your child's bedroom and notice a notebook by her bed titled "My diary—keep out!"**

SHE SAYS

"My diary–keep out!"

YOU MIGHT THINK

"What is she writing that she doesn't want me to see?"

At this age, your child is experiencing a wider range of contradictory feelings. By putting them on paper, she is externalizing, organizing, and processing them, which makes her feel better. She's also learning that she can choose what she shares. By writing "keep out," she's trusting you not to look.

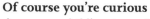

Of course you're curious about your child's private thoughts. You may worry that she has something to hide or that she no longer trusts you, but her diary is part of finding her independent voice as she grows up.

YOUR CHILD IS STARTING TO LEARN THERE CAN BE BOUNDARIES BETWEEN WHAT SHE THINKS AND WHAT SHE TELLS YOU AND OTHER PEOPLE.

WHAT SHE'S THINKING

"I don't want to tell Mommy and Daddy everything. I like having thoughts others don't know about."

A diary is your child's safe place to express all her feelings, including uncomfortable ones such as hatred or jealousy, which are often disapproved of by adults. At this age, your child's writing skills and memory have also improved, so she'll find it exciting that she's now able to create a private space where she can say what she likes freely, without adult censure.

SEE RELATED TOPICS

I hate you!: pp.184–185
You're embarrassing me: pp.206–207

HOW TO RESPOND

In the moment...

Don't read it. If your child finds out you have read her diary, you risk losing her trust. In any case, it's likely to be a basic retelling of the events of her day.

Welcome it. Don't see your child's diary as a way to exclude you. Be pleased that she wants to write about her thoughts, feelings, and experiences. Research has found that keeping a diary reduces stress and improves health.

In the long term...

Talk about good and bad secrets. Explain that a bad secret would make her feel sad, worried, or frightened, whereas a good secret, such as a surprise party or present, would make her feel excited. Emphasize that she needs to talk to a grown-up if she has a bad secret.

Stay connected. Spend unhurried time together so your child has the opportunity to confide in you. Casually ask about her friends. Choose neutral settings to talk, such as in the car or while walking to and from the park. Let her know you are always there when she wants to talk.

Take her concerns seriously. Her problems matter to her, even if they seem small from an adult perspective. Listen and reflect all her feelings, no matter what they are. Ask, "What do you think might help?" instead of leaping in with advice.

"Why do you have to go to work?"

Your child loves you and wants to be with you, so when your job takes you away or intrudes into the time you have together, he may feel disappointed or resentful. For the same reason, he may also ask, "Why do I have to go to school?"

SCENARIO | **You have to leave early to get to work and won't be able to take your child to school.**

HE SAYS

"Why do you have to go to work?"

This question is not a philosophical pondering of the complexities of work-family balance. Your child is just frustrated that you can't do something he wants you to do. He likes it when you take him to school and would protest any obstacle to that.

YOU MIGHT THINK

"I have to do what I have to do."

Every family's solution to managing work and childcare carries pros and cons. If you are matter-of-fact about the solution that works best for your family right now, your child will be, too. Occasional grumbling doesn't necessarily mean there's a problem.

" "

MODEL A POSITIVE ATTITUDE TOWARD WORK, BUT AVOID LETTING IT SPILL INTO FAMILY TIME.

HOW TO RESPOND

In the moment...

Be understanding. Acknowledge his feelings and tell him you wish you could drop him off at school, too. Remember you're both strong enough to survive small disappointments. Make a plan to do something else together, at a different time.

Help your child understand what you do. Bring him to your work, if you can. Let him meet your colleagues. Explain what you enjoy or find interesting about your job, who it helps, and why it matters. Tell him about your workday.

Avoid complaining about your job. One day, your child will also have a job. Try to model for him a positive attitude toward work. If you allow your work to make you tense and irritable, your child will conclude that work is bad.

In the long term...

Be a mindful parent. When you come home, visualize yourself letting go of the workday and embracing your home life. Give your child your full attention when you first come home. Research says daily parent-child reunions can be times of special intimacy.

Beware work spillover. Digital devices can make it hard to have boundaries between work and home. If you must work in the evening, try to wait until your child is in bed.

WHAT HE'S THINKING

"I wish Mommy could always do what I want her to do."

You know all the reasons why you work, but your child only vaguely understands that you go to work, just like he goes to school, and sometimes you can't do what he wants because of work. Your attitude toward your work will influence his.

SEE RELATED TOPICS
I have to tell you something!: pp.178–179
I don't want to go to school: pp.196–197

"You never let me do anything."

At this age, your child may want to start doing new things by herself to feel more grown up or be like her peers. Her wish for independence may lead her to object to your restrictions. You'll need to adjust or hold limits thoughtfully as she grows.

SCENARIO | **After school, your child says her new friend has asked her to come to her dad's house for a sleepover, but you say no.**

SHE SAYS

"You never let me do anything."

YOU MIGHT THINK

"She's still so little. I'm not comfortable with this."

A sleepover sounds exciting. If her friends are going, she won't want to feel left out. But she may or may not actually want to go. She'll protest your "no" on principle, but she may feel relieved by your refusal if she's not ready to sleep over yet.

It's your child's job to test limits and your job to set them. It's important to give your child room to try new experiences, but you also need to make decisions that reflect safety concerns, your values, and your child's current level of maturity.

FIND THE RIGHT BALANCE BETWEEN SAYING YES AND NO TO SUPPORT YOUR CHILD'S GROWING INDEPENDENCE.

WHAT SHE'S THINKING

"All my friends get to go to sleepovers. I'm not a baby."

"Everyone else gets to do it!" is a classic child argument. It's usually not true. But even if it is, you know what's right for your child and your family. Children hate to hear no, but they also feel safe when parents set fair and thoughtful parameters.

HOW TO RESPOND

In the moment...

(1)

Don't be pressured. Give yourself time to think about your decision. If your child asks in front of the other child and begs you to say yes right away, insist, "I need to think about this." You may also want to talk to the other parent before you decide.

(2)

Avoid giving an automatic no. Consider your child's request carefully. Ask questions so you understand the plan. Can you adjust the plan to make it doable? If you decide to say no, try to give her some of what she wants. For instance, maybe she could stay until 10 p.m. to enjoy most of the get-together then come home to sleep in her own bed.

(3)

Explain your decision. It's easier for children to accept no when they understand the reasons behind it. You might say, "We don't know this family well enough" or "You'll sleep better in your own bed." After you explain, don't let her badger you endlessly with "But why not?"

In the long term...

Get to know other parents. You will feel more comfortable letting your child do things with peers if you make a conscious effort to get to know the families of other children in her class.

Respect her need for independence. Look for ways to allow her to do things that feel grown-up. These could include choosing her outfit, decorating her room, trying a new sport, learning to cook something, or planning a get-together with friends.

SEE RELATED TOPICS
It's not fair!: pp.180–181
I wish I had a different family: pp.194–195

"I want a phone."

Although most parents wait until their children reach double digits to give them a phone, with many schools using tablets and laptops, you'll need to figure out your family technology rules sooner rather than later.

SCENARIO | Your child says he really needs a phone for his birthday.

HE SAYS

"I want a phone."

To a child, a phone seems to be the ultimate toy. He wants it to play games, take photos, and send messages, just as you do. He is not yet mature enough to realize that phones can be absorbing and interfere with the in-person interaction, play, and physical activity he needs for healthy development.

YOU MIGHT THINK

"A phone could help keep him safe, but I'm not sure he's old enough for one."

You may be tempted to give your child a phone so you can contact him easily, especially if you and your co-parent live separately. But ask yourself: is he mature enough not to lose or break it? Would it lead to arguments or distract him from other activities?

"

KIDS LOVE GADGETS, BUT ELECTRONIC DEVICES AREN'T A NECESSARY PART OF CHILDHOOD.

WHAT HE'S THINKING

"It would be so cool to have my own phone!"

Smartphones are fascinating and powerful. Your child lives in a world where everyone appears to be on a phone, so it's natural for him to want one, too. He might also think having a phone will impress his friends or allow him to connect with them more.

SEE RELATED TOPICS
No one likes me: pp.190–191
But all my friends have one: pp.208–209

HOW TO RESPOND

In the moment...

Say no. Many children assume that phones are free. They also tend to think that a phone is a right they are entitled to rather than something they have to prove they are ready for. Tell him that phones are expensive and that they are a privilege he may get when he is older.

Ask what he wants to do on a phone. Most likely, he wants to play games, take photos, or message friends. You may be able to find ways to let him do these through limited access to your phone or another device that he doesn't carry with him at all times.

Discuss the downside of technology. When you're out and about, point out people using their phones rather than experiencing or interacting. Explain that devices can be hypnotizing and take away time from sleeping, talking, studying, playing in person, or exploring the world. They can also expose kids to cyberbullying or inappropriate content.

In the long term...

Model balanced phone use. Put your phone away during meals and other family times, to demonstrate good manners and show your child that you value in-person interaction.

Build up gradually. Start your child's access to electronics using a family tablet or computer with parental controls. Let him manage a "dumb" phone before a smartphone. Guide and monitor his activity so he learns to navigate the digital world safely.

"My legs are too fat."

Children are exposed to more images of physical perfection now than in the past. This can make them acutely aware of how their own bodies fall short of imaginary ideals. They need adult guidance to counteract unhealthy societal messages about how they "should" look.

SCENARIO | **Your child is crying because she thinks her legs are fat.**

SHE SAYS

"My legs are too fat."

As children grow up, adults tend to comment on girls' appearance more than boys', who tend to be complimented on assertiveness and strength. It can mean girls grow up thinking that appearance is the most important thing about them. Research shows that even preschoolers worry about being fat.

" "
PARENTS HAVE A KEY ROLE IN MAKING SURE CHILDREN DEVELOP A HEALTHY BODY IMAGE.

I'm the worst: pp.182–183
I'm not as good as them: pp.220–221

YOU MIGHT THINK

"She's beautiful. How can she think such a thing about herself at such a young age?"

Avoid arguing about a certain body part. Instead, question the idea that she "should" look a certain way. Kids' bodies come in all shapes and sizes. Tell your child that she has the body that's right for her.

WHAT SHE'S THINKING

"My body isn't perfect. I feel ugly."

Children used to have a more realistic view of how people looked from just seeing the people around them. In a world where celebrity culture and touched-up photos are everywhere, it's hard for kids to know what's normal or real.

HOW TO RESPOND

In the moment...

Listen first. Ask your child, "What makes you think that?" Maybe someone teased her. Or maybe she doesn't understand how bodies work or that child bodies don't look like adult bodies.

Value other qualities. Compliment her on being kind, creative, funny, determined, or curious. Help her find activities, such as music, art, sports, hobbies, or volunteering, so she knows there's more to her than how she looks. Make sure home is a place where she's loved and accepted as she is.

In the long term...

Be kinder to yourself. Avoid criticizing your appearance—or making comments about others—talking about dieting, or weighing yourself in front of her. If she sees you fretting about your body, she's more likely to worry about hers, regardless of her weight.

Teach media literacy. Explain that images online and in magazines are usually modified. Nobody really looks like that. Look at a magazine together and see if she can recognize real versus fake images of people.

Never criticize your child's body, even in jest. She will encounter plenty of body shaming in the outside world. If your pediatrician says she is overweight, focus on ways to be healthier as a family, such as eating healthy meals at home or going for walks or bike rides together.

After-school activities

After-school lessons and clubs can help kids build on their talents as well as meet new friends with similar interests. Let your child try various ones to find those that appeal to her.

Soccer, tennis, swimming, music, foreign language—there are so many opportunities for children to learn through after-school activities. But don't go overboard. Children need plenty of unstructured time to get together with friends, be with family, or just relax and play on their own.

The activities you choose to explore will depend on your personal values and your child's interests and aptitudes as well as what's available in your community and what's doable for your family. One or two hours per week of activities is plenty for young children.

Don't be surprised if your child's interests shift. Kids are constantly growing and changing. The goal of activities should be for your child to try new things, to become more capable, and most of all to have fun.

> **WHEN CHILDREN FIND AN ACTIVITY THAT DEVELOPS INTO A SKILL, THEY FEEL MORE COMPETENT, WHICH BOOSTS SELF-WORTH.**

1
Start small.
Try a short session to gauge your child's interest before signing her up for a new after-school activity.

4
Ignore FOMO.
When you see other parents signing their kids up for different activities, you may feel a pinch of "fear of missing out" on opportunities for your child. Let it go.

7
Monitor your stress levels.
If you find yourself rushing from one activity to another and are starting to feel overwhelmed, chances are your child is overwhelmed, too.

9
TIY—teach it yourself.
For activities that can easily be done at home—cooking or arts and crafts—your child would probably rather learn by doing them with you.

GOOD PRACTICE

10 key principles

2
Coordinate with other parents.
Children enjoy doing activities with their friends and sharing the car pool load can make things easier for you.

3
Match the activity to your child.
Use your knowledge of your child to pick promising activities. While all kids need physical activity, some love team sports, some prefer dance, and some would rather just run around in the backyard or at the local park.

5
Watch for signs of overload.
If your child seems constantly tired, suffers from frequent tummy- or headaches, or often complains that she wants so stay home, you may need to cut back on activities. Too much of a good thing can be overwhelming for children.

6
Know when to quit.
Sometimes an activity turns out not to be a good fit for your child. Let your child stop and try something else if this doesn't hurt teammates or waste your money. Otherwise, unless the situation is dire, encourage your child to finish the session before shifting to a new activity.

8
Follow your child's lead.
Activities can help children discover and develop their own interests and sense of identity. Stay in the background by making sure your child's enthusiasm for the activity is greater than yours.

10
Give them daily downtime.
A range of studies has found that unstructured play helps children to regulate emotions, make plans, and solve problems. Make sure your child has time every day for free play that does not involve screens.

TAILORED ADVICE

Age by age

2—3
YEARS OLD

One-on-one time
At this age, most children learn better from one-on-one fun interaction with a parent or caregiver than larger group activities. A trip to the park, playing games, and singing nursery rhymes with you is just as rewarding as a structured music class.

4—5
YEARS OLD

Settling in
The start of the school year can be stressful, so you may want to wait a month before adding activities.

Playing first
Prioritize one-on-one playdates. These help your child deepen friendships and practice social skills she can't learn when adults direct the action.

6—7
YEARS OLD

Balancing activities
If your child objects to activities you feel are important for her well-being, such as swim class, church, or speech therapy, it's okay to insist, but explain why they matter. Offer to also do an activity of her choice.

Getting enough sleep?
At this age, children need 9–11 hours of sleep. Cut back on activities if your child is often finishing homework late or going to bed past her bedtime.

References

*All web links accessed July–October 2018.

008–009 FOREWORD
R. E. Larzelere, A. Sheffield, E. Morris, and A. W. Harrist, *Authoritative Parenting: Synthesizing Nurturance and Discipline for Optimal Child Development*, Washington, D.C., APA, 2013.

016–017 WHAT ARE YOUR VALUES?
Values in Action (VIA) Strengths Inventory, www.viacharacter.org.

018–019 BE YOUR CHILD'S EMOTION COACH
L. Gus, J. Rose, and L. Gilbert, "Emotion Coaching: A universal strategy for supporting and promoting sustainable emotional and behavioural well-being," *Educational & Child Psychology* 32 (2015), 31–41.

020–021 A "GOOD ENOUGH" PARENT
E. Ochs and T. Kremer-Sadlik, "The Good Enough Family," in E. Ochs and T. Kremer-Sadlik, (eds.), *Fast-Forward Family: Home, Work, and Relationships in Middle-Class America*, UC Press, 2013, 232–252.
D. W. Winnicott, *The Child, the Family, and the Outside World*, Penguin, 1973.

024–025 HOW CHILDREN LEARN
L. E. Berk, *Child Development*, 9th ed., Pearson, 2012.

026–027 YOUR CHILD'S BRAIN
S. Aamodt and S. Wang, *Welcome to Your Child's Brain*, New York, Bloomsbury, 2011.
T. Payne Bryson and D. Siegel, *The Whole-Brain Child: 12 Proven Strategies to Nurture Your Child's Developing Mind*, London, Robinson, 2012.

028–033 MILESTONES
L. E. Berk, *Child Development*, 9th ed., Pearson, 2012.
"Child Development Tracker," PBS Parents, www.pbs.org/parents/child-development/.
E. Hoff, "Language Experience and Language Milestones During Early Childhood," in K. McCartney and D. Phillips, (eds.), *Blackwell Handbook of Early Childhood Development*, Blackwell, 2005, 233–251.
C. Wood, *Yardsticks: Child and Adolescent Development Ages 4–14*, 4th ed., Center for Responsive Schools, Inc., 2018.

036–037 THAT'S MINE!
N. Chernyak and T. Kushnir, "Giving pre-schoolers choice increases sharing behaviour," *Psychological Science* 24 (2013), 1971–1979.
N. Eisenberg, T. L. Spinrad, and A. Knafo-Noam, "Prosocial development," *Handbook of Child Psychology and Developmental Science*, 2015, 1–47.

038–039 I DO IT!
S. I. Hammond and J. I. M. Carpendale, "Helping children help: The relation between maternal scaffolding and children's early help," *Social Development* 24 (2015), 367–383.

040–041 NO! NO! NO!
K. Österman and K. Björkqvist, "A cross-sectional study of the onset, cessation, frequency, and duration of children's temper tantrums in a nonclinical sample," *Psychological Reports* 106 (2010), 448–454.

042–043 NO BROCCOLI!
L. R. Fries, N. Martin, and K. van der Horst, "Parent-child mealtime interactions associated with toddlers' refusals of novel and familiar foods," *Physiology & Behavior* 176 (2017), 93–100.

044–045 EATING OUT
J. S. Radesky et al., "Patterns of mobile device use by caregivers and children during meals in fast food restaurants," *Pediatrics* (2014), peds-2013.

046–047 BLUE CUP. NO, YELLOW CUP. NO, BLUE CUP.
C. Dauch et al., "The influence of the number of toys in the environment on toddlers' play," *Infant Behavior and Development* 50 (2018), 78–87.

048–049 DADDY, SIT THERE!
K. C. Goffin et al., "A Secure Base from which to Cooperate: Security, Child and Parent Willing Stance, and Adaptive and Maladaptive Outcomes in two Longitudinal Studies," *Journal of Abnormal Child Psychology* 46 (2018), 1061–1075.

050–051 NO COAT!
T. Dix et al., "Autonomy and children's reactions to being controlled: Evidence that both compliance and defiance may be positive markers in early development," *Child Development* 78 (2007), 1204–1221.

052–053 MOMMY, DON'T GO!
C. Altman et al., "Anxiety in early childhood: what do we know?" *Journal of Early Childhood & Infant Psychology* 5 (2009), 157–175.

054–055 HITTING AND BITING
G. F. Freda and A. Dahl, "How Young Children Come to View Harming Others as Wrong: A Developmental Analysis," in *Social Cognition*, Routledge, 2016, 169–202.
P. K. Smith, "Physical activity play: Exercise play and rough-and-tumble," *Children and Play: Understanding Children's Worlds* (2010), 99–123.

056–057 WANT YOUR PHONE!
"What the Research Says About the Impact of Media on Children Under 3 Years Old," Zero to Three [web article], www.zerotothree.org/resources/series/coming-soon-screen-sense.

058–059 I WANT MORE!
C. V. Farrow, E. Haycraft, and J. M. Blissett, "Teaching our children when to eat: how parental feeding practices inform the development of emotional eating—a longitudinal experimental design," *American Journal of Clinical Nutrition* 101 (2015), 908–913.
R. F. Rodgers et al., "Maternal feeding practices predict weight gain and obesogenic eating behaviors in young children," *International Journal of Behavioral Nutrition and Physical Activity* 10 (2013).

060–061 DON'T LIKE HER!
P. S. Klein, R. R. Kraft, and C. Shohet, "Behaviour patterns in daily mother–child separations: possible opportunities for stress reduction," *Early Child Development and Care* 180 (2010), 387–396.
E. Venturelli and A. Cigala, "Daily welcoming in childcare centre as a microtransition," *Early Child Development and Care* 186 (2016), 562–577.

062–063 SHYNESS
J. Kagan, "New insights into temperament," *Cerebrum* 6 (2004), 51–66.
K. H. Rubin, R. J. Coplan, and J. C. Bowker, "Social withdrawal in childhood," *Annual Review of Psychology* 60 (2009), 141–171.

064–065 LET'S PRETEND…
J. A. Blundon and C. E. Schaefer, "The role of parent-child play in children's development," *Psychology and Education* 43 (2006), 1–10.
L. Ma and A. S. Lillard, "The evolutionary significance of pretend play: Two-year-olds' interpretation of behavioral cues," *Learning & Behavior* 45 (2017), 441–448.

066–067 I WANT IT NOW!
K. Imuta, H. Hayne, and D. Scarf, "I want it all and I want it now: delay of gratification in preschool children," *Developmental Psychobiology* 56 (2014), 1541–1552.

068–069 I'M NOT FINISHED
K. C. Radley and E. H. Dart, "Antecedent strategies to promote children's and adolescents' compliance with adult requests," *Clinical Child and Family Psychology Review* 19 (2016), 39–54.

070–071 PLEASE, PLEASE, PLEASE
M. Krcmar et al., "Observing parent-child purchase related interactions in US-based retail environments: replication and extension," *Journal of Children and Media* 11 (2017), 261–277.

072–073 NOT MOMMY. WANT DADDY.
T. Umemura et al., "Do toddlers prefer the primary caregiver or the parent with whom they feel more secure? The role of toddler emotion," *Infant Behavior and Development* 36 (2013), 102–114.

074–075 SLEEP DIFFICULTIES
L. J. Meltzer and V. M. Crabtree, *Pediatric sleep problems: A clinician's guide to behavioral interventions*, APA, 2015.

076–077 WANT THIS STORY
Z. M. Flack, A. P. Field, and J. S. Horst, "The effects of shared storybook reading on word learning," *Developmental Psychology* 54 (2018), 1334–1346.
A. Shahaeian et al., "Early shared reading, socioeconomic status, and children's cognitive and school competencies: Six years of longitudinal evidence," *Scientific Studies of Reading* 22 (2018), pp485–502.

078–079 I LIKE THIS STICK
G. Bento and G. Dias, "The importance of outdoor play for young children's healthy development," *Porto Biomedical Journal* 2 (2017), 157–160.

080–081 WHAT DOES THIS ONE DO?
C. Kidd and B. Y. Hayden, "The psychology and neuroscience of curiosity," *Neuron* 88 (2015), 449–460.

082–083 ONE FOR YOU, ONE FOR ME
C. A. Brownell et al., "Socialization of Early Prosocial Behavior: Parents' Talk about Emotions Is Associated with Sharing and Helping in Toddlers," *Infancy* 18 (2013), 91–119.

084–085 CARVING OUT QUALITY TIME
L. B. Adamson et al., "From interactions to conversations: The development of joint engagement during early childhood," *Child Development* 85 (2014), 941–955.
T. Kremer-Sadlik and A. L. Paugh, "Everyday Moments: Finding 'quality time' in American working families," *Time & Society* 16 (2007), 287–308.

086–087 WHEN IS TOMORROW?
K. A. Tillman and D. Barner, "Learning the language of time: Children's acquisition of duration words," *Cognitive Psychology* 78 (2015), 55–77.

090–091 I WANT A CUDDLE
J. S. Grady, K. Karraker, and A. Metzger, "Shyness trajectories in slow-to-warm-up infants: Relations with child sex and maternal parenting," *Journal of Applied Developmental Psychology* 33 (2012), 91–101.
K. T. Hoffman et al., "Changing toddlers' and preschoolers' attachment classifications: the Circle of Security intervention," *Journal of Consulting and Clinical Psychology* 74 (2006), 1017–1026.

092–093 LOOK WHAT I DID!
S. Harter, *The Construction of the Self: Developmental and Sociocultural Foundations*, New York, Guilford, 2015.

094–095 I WANT MY PACIFIER!
A. M. Nelson, "A Comprehensive Review of Evidence and Current Recommendations Related to Pacifier Usage," *Journal of Pediatric Nursing* 27 (2012), 690–699.

096–097 ARE YOU SAD, MOMMY?
V. L. Castro et al., "Parents' emotion-related beliefs, behaviours, and skills predict children's recognition of emotion," *Infant and Child Development* 24 (2015), 1–22.
R. Ensor, D. Spencer, and C. Hughes, "'You feel sad?' Emotion understanding mediates effects of verbal ability and mother–child mutuality on prosocial behaviors. Findings from 2 years to 4 years," *Social Development* 20 (2011), 93–110.

098–099 I'M SO MAD!
J. J. Gross, "Emotion regulation: taking stock and moving forward," *Emotion* 13 (2013), 359–365.
E. A. Lemerise and B. D. Harper, "The development of anger from preschool to middle childhood: Expressing, understanding, and regulating anger," in *International Handbook of Anger*, New York, Springer, 2010, 219–229.
K. R. Wilson, S. S. Havighurst, and A. E. Harley, "Tuning in to Kids: An effectiveness trial of a parenting program targeting emotion socialization of preschoolers," *Journal of Family Psychology* 26 (2012), 56–65.

100–101 I'M JUST GOING TO DO IT
A. Simpson and D. J. Carroll, "Young children can overcome their weak inhibitory control, if they conceptualize a task in the right way," *Cognition* 170 (2018), 270–279.
M. M. Swingler et al., "Maternal behavior predicts neural underpinnings of inhibitory control in preschoolers," *Developmental Psychobiology* 60 (2018), 692–706.

102–103 THAT'S SO FUNNY!
E. Loizou and M. Kyriakou, "Young children's appreciation and production of verbal and visual humor," *Humor* 29 (2016), 99–124.
C. Lyon, "Humour and the young child: A review of the research literature," *TelevIZIon* 19 (2006), 4–9.

104–105 CAN MR. GIRAFFE SIT DOWN, TOO?
M. Taylor, A. B. Shawber, and A. M. Mannering, "Children's imaginary companions: What is it like to have an invisible friend," *Handbook of Imagination and Mental Simulation* (2009), 211–224.

106–107 MOVING AWAY
F. Mcdway, "Best practices in assisting relocating families," *Best Practices in School Psychology IV* (2002), 1461–1471.
E. Spencer, K. Page, and M. G. Clark, "Managing Frequent Relocation in Families? Considering Prospect Theory, Emotional Framing, and Priming," *Family and Consumer Sciences Research Journal* 45 (2016), 77–90.

108–109 I LOVE BEING WITH YOU
J. Bowlby, *The Making and Breaking of Affectional Bonds*, Abingdon, Routledge, 2005.
M. Sunderland, *The Science of Parenting*, London, Dorling Kindersley, 2008.

110–111 WHY IS THE SKY BLUE?
M. M. Chouinard, "Children's questions: a mechanism for cognitive development," *Monographs of the Society for Research in Child Development* 72 (2007), 1–129.
B. N. Frazier, S. A. Gelman, and H. M. Wellman, "Preschoolers' search for explanatory information within adult-child conversation," *Child Development* 80 (2009), 1592–1611.

112–113 BUT I DIDN'T HEAR YOU
A. Y. Blandon and B. L. Volling, "Parental gentle guidance and children's compliance within the family: A replication study," *Journal of Family Psychology* 22 (2008), 355–366.

114–115 WHEN I WAS LITTLE…
P. J. Bauer, "Development of episodic and autobiographical memory: The importance of remembering forgetting," *Developmental Review*, 38 (2015), 146–166.

116–117 I GIVE UP
M. K. Alvord, B. Zucker, and J. J. Grados, *Resilience Builder Program for children and adolescents*, Research Press, 2011.
C. Dweck, "Carol Dweck revisits the growth mindset," *Education Week* 35 (2015), 20–24.
K. Haimovitz, and C. S. Dweck, "The origins of children's growth and fixed mindsets: New research and a new proposal," *Child Development* 88 (2017), 1849–1859.

118–119 I'M SCARED OF THE DARK
M. Clementi et al., "Treatment of insomnia and nighttime fears," *Comprehensive evidence-based interventions for children and adolescents* (2014), 261–273.
H. Loxton, "Monsters in the dark and other scary things: preschoolers' self-reports," *Journal of Child and Adolescent Mental Health* 21 (2009), 47–60.

120–121 I'M TELLING
G. P. Ingram, "From hitting to tattling to gossip: An evolutionary rationale for the development of indirect aggression," *Evolutionary Psychology* 12 (2014).
I. C. Loke et al., "Children's moral evaluations of reporting the transgressions of peers: Age differences in evaluations of tattling," *Developmental Psychology* 47 (2011), 1757–1762.

122–123 CAR TRIPS
L. H. Koops, "Songs from the car seat: Exploring the early childhood music-making place of the family vehicle," *Journal of Research in Music Education* 62 (2014), 52–65.

124–125 YOU LOVE HER MORE
A. Milevsky, *Sibling Relationships in Childhood and Adolescence. Predictors and Outcomes*, New York, Columbia Univ. Press, 2011.

126–127 I LOST TEDDY
T. Ahluvalia and C. E. Schaefer, "Implications of transitional object use: A review of empirical findings," *Psychology: A Journal of Human Behavior* 31 (1994), 45–57.
C. J. Litt, "Theories of Transitional Object Attachment: An Overview," *International Journal of Behavioral Development* 9 (1986), 383–399.

128–129 YOU'RE ALWAYS TOO BUSY
M. A. Milkie et al., "Time with children, children's well-being, and work-family balance among employed parents," *Journal of Marriage and Family* 72 (2010), 1329–1343.
C. L. Neece, S. A. Green, and B. L. Baker, "Parenting stress and child behavior problems: A transactional relationship across time," *American Journal on Intellectual and Developmental Disabilities* 117 (2012), 48–66.
Pew Research Center, "Raising kids and running a household: How working parents share the load," (2015), www.pewresearch.org.

130–131 I HATE HER
L. Kramer, "The essential ingredients of successful sibling relationships: An emerging framework for advancing theory and practice," *Child Development Perspectives* 4 (2010), 80–86.
A. Siddiqui and H. Ross, "Mediation as a method of parent intervention in children's disputes," *Journal of Family Psychology* 18 (2004), p147.

132–133 I FEEL SAD
D. J. Siegel, "Toward an interpersonal neurobiology of the developing mind: Attachment relationships, 'mindsight,' and neural integration," *Infant Mental Health Journal* 22 (2001), 67–94.
K. R. Wilson, S. S. Havighurst, and A. E. Harley, "Tuning in to Kids: An effectiveness trial of a parenting program targeting emotion socialization of preschoolers," *Journal of Family Psychology* 26 (2012), 56–65.

134–135 I NEVER WANTED A LITTLE BROTHER
B. L. Volling, "Family transitions following the

birth of a sibling: An empirical review of changes in the firstborn's adjustment," *Psychological Bulletin* 138 (2012) 497–528.

136–137 DEALING WITH A SICK CHILD
"Colds in Children," *Paediatrics & Child Health*, 10 (2005), 493–495.
C. Eiser, "Changes in understanding of illness as the child grows," *Archives of Disease in Childhood* 60 (1985), 489–492.

138–139 THEY CALLED ME A CRYBABY
S. P. Mirabile, D. Oertwig, and A. G. Halberstadt, "Parent emotion socialization and children's socioemotional adjustment: when is supportiveness no longer supportive?" *Social Development* 27 (2018), 466 481.
M. B. Scrimgeour, E. L. Davis, and K. A. Buss, "You get what you get and you don't throw a fit!: Emotion socialization and child physiology jointly predict early prosocial development," *Developmental Psychology* 52 (2016), 102–116.

140–141 I HAD A BAD DREAM
M. T. Floress et al., "Nightmare prevalence, distress, and anxiety among young children," *Dreaming* 26 (2016) 280–292.
L. J. Meltzer and V. M. Crabtree, *Pediatric Sleep Problems*, APA, 2015.

142–143 I DIDN'T DO IT
K. Lee et al., "Can classic moral stories promote honesty in children?" *Psychological Science* 25 (2014), 1630–1636.
V. Talwar, C. Arruda, and S. Yachison, "The effects of punishment and appeals for honesty on children's truth-telling behavior," *Journal of Experimental Child Psychology* 130 (2015), 209–217.
V. Talwar and K. Lee, "Emergence of white-lie telling in children between 3 and 7 years of age," *Merrill-Palmer Quarterly* (2002), 160–181.
A. E. Wilson, M. D. Smith, and H. S. Ross, "The nature and effects of young children's lies," *Social Development* 12 (2003), 21–45.

144–145 I HAD AN ACCIDENT
G. G. Peacock, T. Chase, and K. K. Prout, "Evidence-Based Interventions for Elimination Disorders in Children and Adolescents: Enuresis and Encopresis," in L. A. Theodore, (ed.), *Handbook of Evidence-Based Interventions for Children and Adolescents*, 2017, 435–446.

146–147 SHE'S NOT LISTENING
D. W. Chen et al., "Peer conflicts of preschool children: Issues, resolution, incidence, and age-related patterns," *Early Education and Development* 12 (2001), 523–544.
E. Doppler-Bourassa, D. A. Harkins, and C. M. Mehta, "Emerging empowerment: Conflict resolution intervention and preschool teachers' reports of conflict behavior," *Early Education and Development* 19 (2008), 885–906.

148–149 I DON'T WANT TO CLEAN UP
J. C. Laurin and M. Joussemet, "Parental autonomy-supportive practices and toddlers' rule internalization," *Motivation and Emotion* 41 (2017), 562–575.
D. M. Pettygrove et al., "From cleaning up to helping out: Parental socialization and children's early prosocial behavior," *Infant Behavior and Development* 36 (2013), 843–846.

150–151 YOU HAVE TO
J. A. Becker, "Bossy and nice requests: Children's production and interpretation," *Merrill-Palmer Quarterly (1982–)* (1986), 393–413.
A. M. Kołodziejczyk and S. L. Bosacki, "Young-school-aged children's use of direct and indirect persuasion: role of intentionality understanding," *Psychology of Language and Communication* 20 (2016), 292–315.

152–153 YOU CAN'T COME TO MY PARTY
J. E. Burr et al., "Relational aggression and friendship during early childhood: 'I won't be your friend!'" *Early Education & Development* 16 (2005), 161–184.
N. R. Crick et al., "Relational aggression in early childhood: 'You can't come to my birthday party unless...'" *Aggression, Antisocial Behavior, and Violence Among Girls: A Developmental Perspective* (2004), 71–89.

154–155 BIRTHDAY PARTIES
A. J. Clarke, "Consuming children and making mothers: birthday parties, gifts and the pursuit of sameness," *Horizontes antropológicos* 13 (2007), 263–287.
J. D. Woolley and A. M. Rhoads, "Now I'm 3: Young Children's Concepts of Age, Aging, and Birthdays," *Imagination, Cognition and Personality* (2017).

156–157 I DON'T WANT TO
S. E. Woods, R. Menna, and A. J. McAndrew, "The mediating role of emotional control in the link between parenting and young children's physical aggression," *Early Child Development and Care* 187 (2017), 1157–1169.

158–159 I WET THE BED
G. G. Peacock, T. Chase, and K. K. Prout, "Evidence-Based Interventions for Elimination Disorders in Children and Adolescents: Enuresis and Encopresis," in L. A. Theodore, (ed.), *Handbook of Evidence-Based Interventions for Children and Adolescents*, 2017, 435–446.

160–161 WILL BAD PEOPLE HURT US?
M. Clementi et al., "Treatment of insomnia and nighttime fears," *Comprehensive evidence-based interventions for children and adolescents* (2014), 261–273.

162–163 IT FEELS GOOD
C. Mallants and K. Casteels, "Practical approach to childhood masturbation—a review," *European Journal of Pediatrics* 167 (2008), 1111–1117.

164–165 WAS THAT GOOD?
S. Harter, *The Construction of the Self: Developmental and Sociocultural Foundations*, New York, Guilford, 2015.
D. J. Owen, A. M. S. Slep, and R. E. Heyman, "The effect of praise, positive nonverbal response, reprimand, and negative nonverbal response on child compliance: A systematic review," *Clinical Child and Family Psychology Review* 15 (2012), 364–385.

166–167 WHY DID GRANDPA DIE?
G. Panagiotaki et al., "Children's and adults' understanding of death: Cognitive, parental, and experiential influences," *Journal of Experimental Child Psychology* 166 (2018), 96–115.

168–169 YOU PROMISED
K. J. Rotenberg, "The conceptualization of interpersonal trust: A basis, domain, and target framework," in K. J. Rotenberg, (ed.), *Interpersonal Trust During Childhood and Adolescence*, Cambridge University Press, 2010, 8–27.

170–171 SEPARATION AND DIVORCE
B. L. Barber and D. H. Demo, "The kids are alright (at least, most of them): Links between divorce and dissolution and child well-being," in M. A. Fine and J. H. Harvey, (eds.), *Handbook of Divorce and Relationship Dissolution*, New York, Routledge, 2006, 289–311.
M. R. LaGraff, H. E. Stolz, and D. J. Brandon, "Longitudinal Program Evaluation of 'Parenting Apart: Effective Co-Parenting,'" *Journal of Divorce & Remarriage* 56 (2015), 117–136.
H. Westberg, T. S. Nelson, and K. W. Piercy, "Disclosure of Divorce Plans to Children: What the Children Have to Say," *Contemporary Family Therapy* 24 (2002), 525–542.

172–173 I WANT IT TO BE PERFECT
G. L. Flett et al., "Perfectionism in children and their parents: A developmental analysis," in G. L. Flett and P. L. Hewitt, (eds.), *Perfectionism: Theory, Research, and Treatment*, APA, 2002, 89–132.
A. H. Zohar and D. Dahan, "Young Children's Ritualistic Compulsive-Like Behavior and Executive Function: A Cross Sectional Study," *Child Psychiatry & Human Development* 47 (2016), 13–22.

174–175 NO COLORING ON THE WALL
L. E. Berk, *Infants, Children, and Adolescents*, 4th ed., Boston, Allyn & Bacon, 2002.

178–179 I HAVE TO TELL YOU SOMETHING!
A. R. Amicarelli et al., "Parenting differentially influences the development of boys' and girls' inhibitory control," *British Journal of Developmental Psychology* 36, (2018), 371–383.
N. Mellor, "ADHD or attention seeking? Ways of distinguishing two common childhood problems," *British Journal of Special Education* 36 (2009) 25–34.

180–181 IT'S NOT FAIR!
M. Johnston and H. Saltzstein, "'That's Not Fair!' Children's Judgments of Maternal Fairness and Good/Bad Intentions," *Journal of Social, Behavioral, and Health Sciences* 10 (2016), 82–92.

182–183 I CAN'T DO IT
B. O. Hier and K. E. Mahony, "The Contribution of Mastery Experiences, Performance Feedback, and Task Effort to Elementary-Aged Students' Self-Efficacy in Writing," *School Psychology Quarterly* 33 (2018), 408–418.
K. Muenks, A. Wigfield, and J. S. Eccles, "I can do this! The development and calibration of children's expectations for success and competence beliefs," *Developmental Review* 48 (2018), 24–39.
C. Wei et al., "Parenting behaviors and anxious self-talk in youth and parents," *Journal of Family Psychology* 28 (2014), 299–307.

184–185 I HATE YOU!
P. Donahue, "Parenting Through Difficult Moments," in S. Tuber, (ed.), *Parenting: Contemporary Clinical Perspectives*, Lanham (MD), Rowman & Littlefield, 2016, 115–137.
J. Zeman, C. Perry-Parrish, and M. Cassano, "Parent-child discussions of anger and sadness: The importance of parent and child gender during middle childhood," *New Directions for Child and Adolescent Development* 2010 (2010), 65–83.

186–187 BUT MOMMY SAID I COULD
J. Jenkins and J. M. Buccioni, "Children's

understanding of marital conflict and the marital relationship," The Journal of Child Psychology and Psychiatry and Allied Disciplines 41 (2000), 161–168.

188–189 GOOD MANNERS
E. Cook and R. Dunifron, "Do Family Meals Really Make a Difference?" Parenting in Context, Cornell University College of Human Ecology, 2012, www. human. cornell. edu.
J. H. Gralinski and C. B. Kopp, "Everyday rules for behavior: Mothers' requests to young children," Developmental Psychology 29 (1993), 573–584.
M. R. Skeer et al., "Going Beyond Frequency: A Qualitative Study to Explore New Dimensions for the Measurement of Family Meals," Journal of Child and Family Studies 27 (2018), 1075–1087.

190–191 NO ONE LIKES ME
B. Laursen, B. D. Finkelstein, and N. T. Betts, "A developmental meta-analysis of peer conflict resolution," Developmental Review 21 (2001), 423–449.
K. H. Rubin et al., "11 Peer Relationships in Childhood," The Oxford Handbook of Developmental Psychology Vol. 2: Self and Other 2 (2013), 242–275.

192–193 THEY'RE BEING MEAN TO ME
E. Menesini and C. Salmivalli, "Bullying in schools: the state of knowledge and effective interventions," Psychology, Health & Medicine 22 (2017), 240–253.

194–195 I WISH I HAD A DIFFERENT FAMILY
H. Omer, "Helping parents deal with children's acute disciplinary problems without escalation: The principle of nonviolent resistance," Family Process 40 (2001), 53–66.

196–197 I DON'T WANT TO GO TO SCHOOL
C. A. Kearney and K. K. Sheldon, "Evidence-based interventions for school refusal behavior in children and adolescents," L. A. Theodore (ed.), Handbook of Evidence-Based Interventions for Children and Adolescents, New York, Springer, 2017, 279–288.

198–199 SHE'S MY BEST FRIEND
F. Poulin and A. Chan, "Friendship stability and change in childhood and adolescence," Developmental Review 30 (2010), 257–272.
A. M. Sebanc et al.., "Predicting having a best friend in young children: Individual characteristics and friendship features," The Journal of Genetic Psychology 168 (2007), 81–96.

200–201 SCHOOL PRESSURE
A. S. Dimech and R. Seiler, "Extra curricular sport participation: A potential buffer against social anxiety symptoms in primary school children," Psychology of Sport and Exercise 12 (2011), 347–354.
K. Fisher et al., "Playing around in school: Implications for learning and educational policy," in A. Pellegrini, (ed.), The Oxford Handbook of Play, New York, Oxford University Press, 2011, 341–363.
S. Harter, The Construction of the Self: Developmental and Sociocultural Foundations, New York, Guilford, 2015.

201–203 HOMEWORK IS BORING
D. Pino-Pasternak, "Applying an observational lens to identify parental behaviours associated with children's homework motivation," British

Journal of Educational Psychology 84 (2014), 352–375.

204–205 I'M THE BEST
E. Brummelman and S. Thomaes, "How Children Construct Views of Themselves: A Social-Developmental Perspective," Child Development 88 (2017), 1763–1773.

206–207 YOU'RE EMBARRASSING ME
S. N. Chobhthaigh and C. Wilson, "Children's understanding of embarrassment: Integrating mental time travel and mental state information," British Journal of Developmental Psychology 33 (2015), 324–339.

208–209 BUT ALL MY FRIENDS HAVE ONE
L. N. Chaplin and D. R. John, "Growing up in a Material World: Age Differences in Materialism in Children and Adolescents," Journal of Consumer Research 34 (2007), 480–493.

210–211 I'M THE WORST
S. Harter, The Construction of the Self: Developmental and Sociocultural Foundations, New York, Guilford, 2015.

212–213 MONEY MATTERS
A. F. Furnham, "Parental attitudes towards pocket money/allowances for children," Journal of Economic Psychology 22 (2001), 397–422.
L. Kiang et al., "If children won lotteries: materialism, gratitude and imaginary windfall spending," Young Consumers 17 (2016), 404–418.

214–215 STOP FIGHTING!
P. T. Davies et al., "A process analysis of the transmission of distress from interparental conflict to parenting: Adult relationship security as an explanatory mechanism," Developmental Psychology 45 (2009), 1761–1773.

216–217 BUT I'M NOT TIRED
M. Hirshkowitz et al., "National Sleep Foundation's sleep time duration recommendations: methodology and results summary," Sleep Health 1 (2015), 40–43.
L. J. Meltzer and V. M. Crabtree, Pediatric Sleep Problems: A Clinician's Guide to Behavioral Interventions, APA, 2015.

218–219 I'M BORED
E. Rhodes, "The exciting side of boredom," The Psychologist 28 (2015), 278–281.

220–221 I'M NOT AS GOOD AS THEM
K. Haimovitz and C. S. Dweck, "The origins of children's growth and fixed mindsets: New research and a new proposal," Child Development 88 (2017), 1849–1859.
A. Lohbeck and J. Möller, "Social and dimensional comparison effects on math and reading self-concepts of elementary school children," Learning and Individual Differences 54 (2017), 73–81.

222–223 I'VE GOT A BOYFRIEND
C. L. Martin, R. A. Fabes, and L. D. Hanish, "Differences and similarities: The dynamics of same- and other-sex peer relationships," in W. M. Bukowski, B. Laursen, and K. H. Rubin, (eds.), Handbook of Peer Interactions, Relationships, and Groups, New York, Guilford, 2018, 391–409.

224–225 I'M NOT PLAYING ANYMORE!
R. Ensor et al., "Gender differences in children's

problem behaviours in competitive play with friends," British Journal of Developmental Psychology 29 (2011), 176–187.
C. Hughes, A. L. Cutting, and J. Dunn, "Acting nasty in the face of failure? Longitudinal observations of 'hard-to-manage' children playing a rigged competitive game with a friend," Journal of Abnormal Child Psychology 29 (2001), 403–416.

226–227 THE DIGITAL WORLD
"The Common Sense Census: Media Use by Kids Age Zero to Eight," Common Sense Media, 2017, www.commonsensemedia.org.
S. Livingstone et al., "Children's online activities, risks and safety: A literature review by the UKCCIS Evidence Group," UKCCIS, 2017.

228–229 WHERE DO BABIES COME FROM?
N. Stone, R. Ingham, and K. Gibbins, "'Where do babies come from?' Barriers to early sexuality communication between parents and young children," Sex Education 13 (2013), 228–240.

230–231 DO I HAVE TO DO MUSIC PRACTICE?
G. E. McPherson, "The role of parents in children's musical development," Psychology of Music 37 (2009), 91–110.

232–233 WHAT'S A STRANGER?
"Staying safe away from home," NSPCC, www. nspcc.org.uk.

234–235 MY DIARY—KEEP OUT!
E. N. Palmer and D. Bowers, "New Twist on a Classic Tool: Using a Journal as a Technique for Organizing Therapy with Young Children," Journal of Family Psychotherapy 26 (2015), 15–18.

236–237 WHY DO YOU HAVE TO GO TO WORK?
R. L. Repetti and S. W. Wang, "Employment and parenting," Parenting 14 (2014), 121–132.

238–239 YOU NEVER LET ME DO ANYTHING
M. Joussemet, R. Landry, and R. Koestner, "A self-determination theory perspective on parenting," Canadian Psychology/Psychologie canadienne 49 (2008), 194–200.

240–241 I WANT A PHONE
K. Chan, "Development of materialistic values among children and adolescents," Young Consumers 14 (2013), 244–257.

242–243 MY LEGS ARE TOO FAT
American Psychological Association, Report of the APA Task Force on the Sexualization of Girls, 2008.
L. Papadopoulos, Sexualisation of Young People Review, UK Home Office, 2010.

244–245 AFTER-SCHOOL ACTIVITIES
J. L. Mahoney, A. L. Harris, and J. S. Eccles, "The Over-Scheduling Myth," Child Trends 12 (2008).

Index

CONTRIBUTING EDITOR

Eileen Kennedy-Moore, PhD, is a clinical psychologist based in Princeton, NJ, and a mom of four. Her books include *Growing Friendships*, *Kid Confidence*, *Smart Parenting for Smart Kids*, and *The Unwritten Rules of Friendship*. A trusted expert on parenting and child development, Dr. Kennedy-Moore serves on the advisory board for *Parents* magazine, and has been a guest on the *Today Show*. She is often quoted in publications such as *Parents*, *Real Simple*, *Working Mother*, the *Wall Street Journal*, the *Chicago Tribune*, and the *New York Times*. Her blog on Psychology Today has more than 2.5 million views. Learn more at EileenKennedyMoore.com, GrowingFriendshipsBlog.com, and DrFriendtastic.com (for kids).

THE AUTHOR

Tanith Carey is an award-winning UK journalist and author who writes on the most pressing challenges facing today's parents. Her eight previous books have been translated into 15 languages, including German, Arabic, and Chinese. Having spent time working in the US as an editor and writer before returning to the UK, Tanith has insight on both sides of the Atlantic and her writing has featured in a wide range of publications including the *Daily Telegraph*, the *Times*, the *Guardian*, and *New York Daily News*. Tanith also appears on TV and radio programs, such as *NBC Today*. Tanith has two daughters.

UK CONSULTANT

Dr. Angharad Rudkin is a UK clinical psychologist and Associate Fellow of the British Psychological Society. She has worked with children, adolescents, and families for over 15 years. Angharad has an independent therapy practice and teaches Clinical Child Psychology at the University of Southampton. She contributes to articles on child and family well-being for national newspaper and magazines. Angharad appears on TV and radio regularly as an expert on child and family issues.

ACKNOWLEDGMENTS

From Eileen Kennedy-Moore Thank you to my husband, Tony, and my children, Mary, Daniel, Sheila, and Brenna. You are my loves, my delight, and my reason for everything. Thank you to the families I've worked with in my clinical psychology practice. I feel honored by the trust you've placed in me and inspired by your journeys. Thank you also to my US DK editors, Lori Hand and Jennette ElNaggar. Finally, thank you to my agent, Betsy Amster, for your wisdom and advocacy.

From Tanith Carey Thanks to my children, Lily and Clio, who made this possible. This is the book I was looking for when you were small and hope you will find it insightful if you have your own children. I learned from you both. Also love to my husband, Anthony, whose support allowed me to take the time to write this book. A special mention must also go to wonderful agent Caroline Montgomery and, of course, Dr. Angharad Rudkin, my calm, wise, and always reasonable consultant, whose first priority has always been to help parents understand their children better. Finally, it's not easy to produce a parenting book that is truly original and also as accessible and user-friendly as this one—and the London DK staff behind this project have been fantastic. What a team.

From Angharad Rudkin Thank you Gwenda and Arthur for wrapping up my childhood with such love and belief, and thank you to David, Nora, Bridget and Arthur who have taught me more than any textbook could.

From the publisher We would like to acknowledge the following in the production of this book: Dr. Angharad Rudkin for developing and planning the book with Tanith Carey; Kathy Steer for proofreading; and Vanessa Bell and Cheryl Lenser for indexing.